OUT *of the* OVERFLOW

Stories of God's Love from His Heart to Yours

OVER 100 CONTRIBUTORS INCLUDING FLORENCE LITTAUER, BRUCE WILKINSON, PAM FARREL, AND JOHN VAN DIEST

WinePress Publishing
Your Book, Defined. Since 1991.

WinePress Publishing, PO Box 428, Enumclaw, WA 98022) functions only as book publisher. As such, the ultimate design, content, editorial accuracy, and views expressed or implied in this work are those of the author.

Out of the Overflow cover art was created by Debbie Hannah Skinner. Through words and images, Debbie helps women find wisdom in Scripture to build stronger relationships—with the Lord and with the ones they love. She's is an artist, speaker, and writer who paints as she speaks, sharing the wisdom of Scripture through water media paintings. Visit her website for more information: www.WisdomInWatercolor.com

Imagery on the cover image:

The colors in this limited palette painting were all chosen for a reason... Green symbolizes fresh, new growth.

Turquoise water represents the Holy Spirit's work in refreshing our spirits then flowing out of us to bless and refresh others.

The terra cotta colored pot is a reminder that we are like clay vessels, formed by God, the Master Potter, and used for His glory.

ISBN 13: 978-1-60615-104-4
ISBN 10: 1-60615-104-5
Library of Congress Catalog Card Number: 2010940416

Special thanks to
Gerry Wakeland, President of CLASSEMINARS, Inc,
WinePress Publishing, and all the authors, mentors, and
editors who contributed to this book.

Out of the Overflow is dedicated to Dan Penwell, former editor at AMG Publishers. Dan always went the extra mile to help writers learn to write with excellence. Many writers in this book were privileged to learn from Dan Penwell. He was our teacher, mentor, encourager, and friend. Dan's influence lives on as writers continue to benefit from his expertise and encouragement. Thank you, Dan, for loving us enough to reject most of us and to publish a select few. Truly he is missed in the publishing world today.

A portion of the proceeds of this book will go to the Dan Penwell Scholarship Fund of CLASSEMINARS, Inc.

"...out of the overflow of the heart, the mouth speaks."

—Luke 6:45

Contents

INTRODUCTION

IN LUKE 6:45 we read, "…out of the overflow of the heart, the mouth speaks." If we hold this to be true, as Christian writers we realize we must be filled to overflowing—spilled out, splashing over, bubbling forth—with God's love onto all those we touch with our words, our works, and our writing.

In November 2010 about 140 Christian writers gathered on the high desert of the famed Ghost Ranch in Abiquiu, New Mexico, for the CLASS Christian Writers Conference. Though their purpose was to learn more of the writing process from esteemed editors, agents, and professional colleagues, their passion and portent was to meet our Lord Jesus Christ and to hear from Him.

While they attended workshops, heard keynote speakers, and networked with industry leaders, the greatest activity was the hours spent in awe and worship, praise, and prayer.

Christian communicators provide hope, encouragement, instruction, inspiration, and information all wrapped up in the unique messages God has given each one to share. The best way to provide this is "out of the overflow." Staying connected to God, studying His Word, spending time with Him in prayer and fellowship, He will fill us so that we will splash out on all we come in contact with. For as He fills our hearts, our mouths will speak and our pens will write and lives will be changed.

From this mindset, or "heart-set," God's blessings spilled out, splashed over, and flowed into their words, ways, and writing. These are a few of their amazing stories, out of the overflow of God's heart to yours. As you read them may the overflow of God's love in the lives of the authors spill over and encourage you.

Bruce Wilkinson

THE JABEZ PRAYER

"And Jabez called on the God of Israel saying, 'Oh, that You would bless me indeed, and enlarge my territory, that Your hand would be with me, and that You would keep me from evil, that I may not cause pain!' So God granted him what he requested."

—1 Chronicles 4:10 (NKJV)

WHEN WAS THE last time God worked through you in such a way that you knew beyond doubt that God had done it? In fact, when was the last time you saw miracles happen on a regular basis in *your* life? If you're like most believers I've met, you wouldn't know how to ask for that kind of experience, or even if you should.

What I have to share with you has been opening up lives to God's mighty working for many years. Recently, I was in Dallas to teach on the Jabez blessings to an audience of 9,000. Later over lunch, a man said to me, "Bruce, I heard you preach the message of Jabez fifteen years ago, and I haven't stopped praying it. The change has been so overwhelming I have just never stopped."

Across the table, another friend agreed. He said he'd been praying Jabez's little prayer for ten years with similar results. The man next to him, from Indianapolis, said he'd been praying it for five.

I told them, "Friends, I've been praying Jabez for more than half my life!"

Because you're reading this book, I believe you share my desire to reach for a life that will be "more honorable" for God. Not that you wish others to reach for less, but for you, nothing but God's fullest blessing will do. When you stand before Him to give your accounting, your deepest desire is to hear, "Well done!"

God really does have unclaimed blessings waiting for you, my friend. I know it sounds impossible—even embarrassingly suspicious in our self-serving day. Yet that very exchange—your want for God's plenty - has been His loving will for your life from eternity past. And with a handful of core commitments on your part, you can proceed from this day forward with the confidence and expectation that your heavenly Father will bring it to pass for you.

Think of it this way: Instead of standing near the river's edge, asking for a cup of water to get you through each day; you'll do something unthinkable - you will take the little prayer with the giant prize and *jump into the river*! At that moment, you will begin to let the loving currents of God's grace and power carry you along. God's great plan for you will surround you and sweep you forward into the profoundly important and satisfying life He has waiting.

Excerpted from *The Prayer of Jabez* by Bruce Wilkinson

Bruce Wilkinson is the author of more than 60 books translated into 30 languages. He has had several books to reach the number one spot on the bestseller lists. *The Prayer of Jabez* remains the fastest selling book in history with worldwide sales exceeding 20 million. Bruce and his wife Darlene have three children and six grandchildren.

Amanda May

Thoughts from a Super Hero

EVERY MORNING BEGINS the same way. I wake up to the sound of my four-year-old whispering, "Mommy, I can't find my sword." He simply can't imagine leaving the fortress of his bedroom unprepared for the dragons that must be faced each day.

Scene II is quickly set with the lamenting of my two-year-old because he will not be able to wear his batman shirt today. Once again his mother has not finished the laundry.

The perspective of my boys always declares them to be Super Heroes. The dragons that hide behind our couch, to the "bad guys" who lurk in the hallway closet ensure that they must always be equipped with their swords in hand, capes properly fit around their neck, and guns nestled in the back of their shirts. Perspective is a funny thing. It dictates your day, drives your passions, and determines your emotions and thoughts. When I choose to put the dishrag down and join in their antics and squeals, I find my perspective merging with theirs.

Kingdom perspective, now that is food for thought. To live in a world that is not consumed by my own egocentric motivations. To know that with every sunrise, I am joining in a battle, equipped or not, that has been waging for generations. As I mature in my relationship with the Lord, He is revealing more of how every book in His Word is a lesson on perspective. Showing me all of the areas in my heart where I have lost His vision, and foolishly traded the space that He designed to only be filled by Him for things that have no eternal value. Perspective, if I dared to ask the Lord, would I think He would say His perspective is more like mine or my boys? I know His lessons in perspective come so freely when I am looking. Like the time I was jogging and heard God clearly tell me to say something to a woman I randomly passed. My perspective on obedience changed. Or when I heard the Lord tell me to give money to a beggar on the street, and I quickly diluted His thoughts for rationalizations of what I needed the money for. As I passed the man in my car, I offered a brief "rooftop" prayer for the Lord to bless him. Upon hearing His calming yet wall shattering voice say "I just tried to," my perspective on my purpose as a servant changed.

Those are the moments where I can almost feel the Holy Spirit giving me my own sword, cape and gun to put on. Maybe the Lord's perspective is more focused on me wearing the sword, cape, and gun, than trying to pick them up and put them back up where they go. Is it too late for me to be a Super Hero? That must be why Jesus came. To invite me to a party that I didn't even know existed. Perspective, it is a paradigm shift that can only occur from the overflow of revelation from our Heavenly Father. Perspective, when morning comes oh Lord, may it be my voice you hear whispering, "God, I can't find my sword."

Amanda May is a wife and mother of two boys. She is a pediatric Physical Therapist, serves with her husband in college ministry leadership, and teams with her mother in writing children's books that reflect the Father's heart. She loves adventures with her family, songwriting, and pursuing God's voice.

Daphne Delay

GOD IS FAITHFUL

AS I STOOD by his bed in ICU, he was unrecognizable. Moments earlier, the nurse showed us a colored diagram of the percent of his burns. She said, "His age will help him. We add his age to his percent of severe burns to determine his mortality rate." I thought, "Did I hear her right… mortality rate? "At my son's side, I could barely process this information.

Benjamin had been with us for Father's Day. On his way back to college, he helped move a friend to Tulsa. Their truck grazed a guardrail and in a freak accident, it flipped and caught on fire in mid-air. Both boys escaped, but Benjamin was trapped in his seatbelt. Miraculously, he managed to pull himself out—but not before receiving third degree burns on most of his right side. The deputies on scene reported they had never before found survivors of such a horrific accident.

I had stood by the bedside of many critical patients before. As pastors, my husband and I had been called in to pray with and encourage the faith of families in desperate situations. We have reminded loved ones of God's faithfulness to His Word and comforted families and individuals with hope and peace despite all odds. Many situations turned into triumphant testimonies, while some left us with nagging thoughts of "Why God?" And with no sure answer in our pastoral role we prayed *for "peace that passes understanding"* for all involved.

But this time, I wasn't the pastor—I was the parent. If I could believe for others and not for myself, doesn't that make God's Word a lie? I could not allow my faith to change just because it was now my son in the bed.

There is only one of two things a parent can do in this situation. Either have faith in God or carry a burden of worry and fear. I could not do both. Thankfully, I had hidden

God's Word in my heart (first for myself, and secondly for others); and it now brought great comfort to me. David was right when he said, "Unless Your law had been my delight, I would then have perished in my affliction" (Psalm 119:92).

We were told to expect Benjamin to be hospitalized for some time. He was on a ventilator to help heal the damage to his lungs and throat after breathing in the fire, and skin graft surgeries were a certainty. His burns covered multiple joint areas, which meant therapy and possible loss of mobility. Benjamin was a talented drummer with a great future, so this news was almost unacceptable—although you couldn't downplay the fact that *he was alive* and we'd face tomorrow together whatever it may be.

Each night, my husband and I were forced to leave ICU. We found comfort in being by our son's bedside looking for any and all signs of improvement. As human as we were, we looked at each other and made the same statement night after night: "Tell me he's going to be okay."

Despite a swirl of emotions, I was reminded of Abraham's faith and how *"...contrary to hope, in hope [he] believed" (Romans 4:18)*. Now was my moment of truth. As any mother would, I cried as I looked at my broken child. Yet in that moment, I made a decision: I will not cry for tomorrow... for God's Word is true and His faithfulness shall be my strength.

The next day, I wrote in my journal: "I am fully convinced of God's Word. We will have victory in the midst of this trial. I have not lost heart because I am confident I will see the goodness of the Lord in the land of the living (Psalm 27:13). Just as Abraham chose not to rely only on "natural" hope (what you can do based on what others are saying), but instead chose to believe according to "spiritual" hope (what GOD can DO based on what HE HAS SAID) - I have chosen the same."

Seven weeks and six surgeries later, Benjamin was released from the hospital. He had endured a tracheotomy and many painful skin grafts. The road ahead would be long, but we all agreed it was what we had stored in our hearts prior to the accident that sustained us. Benjamin is now playing the drums as he heals. And more than ever, my heart says, "God is faithful."

Daphne Delay is an ordained minister and Bible Teacher. As the founder of Mirror Ministries, she has authored and self-published two books on righteousness and written over 200 articles on spiritual growth for her readers. She is a regular contributor for CBN.com and her articles are published weekly in three Texas newspapers. www.mirrorministries.org

Caleb Jennings Breakey

Love and Legacy

WRITER'S NOTE: This poem is dedicated to my grandpa, Raymond Jennings Breakey (Pop-Pop), who passed away on September 11 at the age of 89 after a battle with cancer. A man whom words fail to capture . . .

Let me show you, Pop-Pop, all your family 'round your bed.
Can you hear us whispering? We're snuggled by your head.

Your eyes are squinted open, you're breathing through this mask.
Yet nothing's ever stopped you, not a mountain, not a task.

I really can't believe my eyes, this scene is nothing true.
How can life go on tomorrow, without the never-changing you?

You never asked for anything, just did what needed done.
Your gentle eyes subdued us, your stories always fun.

You've loved your family in a way most other men can't claim;
you've toiled long and hard for us, not once you spoke of pain.

I want to hold your hand forever, can't let go of who you are.
You're everybody's favorite, Pop-Pop, you're everybody's star.

The way you watched us Christmas morning, rockin' your old brown leather chair;
you invested love in each of us—Pop, this isn't fair.

Can't we have more time with you, a day to show our love?
How can this be the hour, for you to meet the One above?

We know your heart is slowing, doctor says it hardly beats;
I find there's nothing greater now than warming your cold feet.

How can I give what you gave to me? I've wasted so much time.
All the great-great love between us seemed always on your dime.

My tears are overtaking, my mouth it quivers strong;
how long have you been hurting, have I missed it all along?

I press my lips close to your ears, I know that you can hear;
God sent his Son for sinners, Pop-Pop, ask Him to come near.

They say they must now take you, my eyes they sting of red;
I pray to the Lord Jesus that your soul is fully fed.

From today shall come tomorrow, and tomorrow we must cope;
we hurt and cry and grieve for you, yet cling to precious hope.

As we hold each other closely, Pop-Pop, our hearts they ache anew;
for we are a love and legacy, and we are because of you.

Caleb Jennings Breakey is an award-winning journalist, editor, book reviewer, speaker, and Christian Writers Guild Craftsman. He operates CalebBreakey.com, where he refines "Teen Writers into Rockstars" via video blogs, audio edits, interviews, contests and more. During the evenings, Caleb works on his two novels alongside his wife, Brittney.

Florence Littauer

BUBBLES IN THE BATHTUB

PICTURE FOR A moment a bathtub. It's empty, cold and hard. Now turn on the faucet and adjust it to the perfect temperature for you. Something cold is warming up. Now pour in some bubble bath, and suddenly the ordinary becomes exciting. The aroma is pleasant, but the best part is watching the bubbles grow. Out of one tablespoon of liquid comes a mountain of bubbles. So, little becomes much. The stronger the force of the water of the water the bigger the bubbles become. Is there anyone of us who can resist the temptation of jumping into such pleasure?

Some of you may want to go right now and start running the water, throw in some bath beads, hop in, and continue to read. But what happens if you get called to the phone before you get in the tub? You shut off the faucet and leave the warm bubbles that may have mounded even higher than the tub itself, intending to come right back. However, the cares of the world detain you and when you return, the fluff and the fun have gone out of the bubbles. They've died down a bit, and many have disappeared forever. But all is not lost. You turn on the water again full force, and with the new encouragement fresh bubbles appear. The water gets warm again. You've revived what seemed to be dying.

Now consider our childhood minds. We've each been given at least a cupful of creativity. Left in the bottle it doesn't produce new ideas, but poured out into a warm environment it begins to bubble. The stronger the encouragement, the fuller the force, the more bubbles appear. So many little children are just bubbling over with enthusiasm and excitement, their minds overflowing with creative thoughts. But what happens if we get left alone with no one stirring up the waters, no one keeping the bubbles alive? After a while the enthusiasm cools down. The bubbles burst and we're left with just a tub of cold water and perhaps the remnant of a few tiny bubbles here and there. But don't despair. We can turn the tap on again. We can bring some of the bubbles back to life. They won't be as big or as lively, but they can be stirred up one more time.

Taken from *The Gift of Encouraging Words*, Word Publishing, 1995

Florence Littauer is the Founder of CLASS (Christian Leaders Authors Speakers Seminars). Teaching the concepts of the personalities for over forty years, her insightful teachings have become the standard in understanding relationships among families, churches, schools, and businesses. Author of more than 40 books and speaker to thousands, Florence knows the importance of communicating with excellence.

Tom Davis

Room for One More

MY WIFE AND I were flat broke. If those were God's words, if it was His voice speaking to us, it didn't matter. We were only twenty-two and twenty-six years old. Where would we find the money to adopt a little girl from Russia? He would make a way, even if all the roads were filled with obstacles.

A seed was planted the summer we led a youth-group mission trip to Vladimir, Russia, to minister to one hundred and fifty orphans. After two weeks with those kids, our lives were challenged in ways we never dreamed possible. God spoke to us through a little brown-eyed Russian orphan.

So there we were, broke and trusting God. It was out of our hands.

I have a feeling you won't be surprised by what I'm going to say next … God did provide. It was His idea in the first place, after all.

We did our part sorting through mountains of paperwork and certified documents, making dozens of phone calls, and talking endlessly with INS (Immigration and Naturalization Service) officers. Eventually, we were ready to finalize the adoption of our little girl, Anya.

I flew to Russia in March to let her know the good news; we would bring her home in June. My heart skipped a few beats and I felt I was living in a dream. I couldn't wait to see this little fatherless girl and tell her she would have a family, and a father, for the rest of her life.

Snow was falling in sheets that day, turning the dirty brown landscape into a cotton white winter wonderland. When our emerald green van pulled up to Yuriev Polsky on that cold spring day, I was bursting with anticipation to see my new daughter.

I opened the creaky, oversized wooden door and stepped into a small foyer where I wiped my feet. Another door stared at me from the foyer. One step through that threshold and I would see Anya, our daughter. What would I find inside? Would Anya say yes? Would she want to come home with us?

The staircase and hallway were lined with children. They stood against the walls, leaned on the railing, and crowded the back of the room. My visit was not a secret. Hundreds of tiny eyes watched my every move.

I looked at the children, they looked at me, none of us sure what to do. Like bullets, two little girls shot toward me. It happened so fast, I didn't have time to react. One grabbed my right leg, the other, my left. They wrapped their arms around me and squeezed tight. One of them started rubbing my leg as if I were a favorite stuffed animal. Her big blue beautiful eyes looked up at me, and she spoke. It was just one word. With every repetition, knives punctured my heart.

"Papa," she said. "Papa, Papa, Papa …"

Air stuck in my throat. I wanted to say something to let her know she was special, that she had significance; she didn't deserve to be rejected. But she was not Anya. She was not the girl I would be soon calling my daughter. All those two little girls wanted was the chance to have a family.

The desperation, the hope, and the love they desired and deserved were all too much for me to process. I decided right then, in that orphanage, I would do whatever I could to help orphaned boys and girls around the world who were hoping against hope that someone would love them. I knew I couldn't adopt seventy children (although it did cross my mind), so what could I do?

I made a commitment to help the organization that exposed me to the needs in Russia. I called my friends, raised money, and took countless trips, all in an attempt to do whatever I could to help orphans like the two little girls who wouldn't let go. That very year, my church sponsored an entire orphanage of kids. The programs we helped establish gave them a hope and a future.

Today, my entire life is about bringing awareness of the orphan's plight to the body of Christ, the secular world, to whoever will listen and help the least of these. Why? Because they're worth it. Every little boy or girl who sits alone, feeling rejected and abandoned by the world, deserves to know they have a Father in heaven who loves them and there are people who care and love them too.

God has a passionate love for the fatherless—the people He calls widows, strangers, and orphans. Our involvement, in the lives of the fatherless can reap huge benefits in their lives. We are Jesus' hands and feet.

Perhaps your path will be through adoption, but there are many other ways to respond—through advocacy, sponsorship, letter writing, taking a trip to visit orphans, or starting a group committed to making a difference in your community.

But whatever you do, do it now because those two precious girls weren't just holding onto my legs—they were holding tight to the hope only you can give them.

Tom Davis is the author of *Fields of the Fatherless, Scared—A Novel on the Edge of the World,* and *Priceless*. He is President and CEO of Children's Hope Chest, a global orphan advocacy organization serving orphans and widows around the world.

Linda L. Boyd

A Gift I Will Never Forget

I WALKED DOWN the hallway of the convalescent hospital and entered the room where my dad lay. He looked frail. As his body had grown weaker with each passing day, his skin clung tightly to his bones. His once vigorous, robust, 6'1" frame was now a mere 115 lbs. For the tenth week in a row I had left my job after work on Friday afternoon and driven from Southern California to Auburn, north of Sacramento. I then made the six-hour return trip every Sunday evening.

When I walked in the room, his beautiful blue eyes twinkled. "There you are, Baby Doll!"

My heart warmed, hearing the term of endearment he had called me throughout my lifetime. "Yes, Daddy, I'm here." I sat next to him, taking his hand in mine.

Within moments it was apparent the pain of a bladder infection was sweeping through him like a violent wave. He tightened his fists to ride out the pain. As it increased, he clenched his teeth and swung his head from side to side as if to say "No" to the unending torment.

Throughout the day, I held his hand and stroked his forehead. More pain ravaged his body as each wave rolled over him. Each time I asked, "Dad, are you alright?" Through most of the day he replied he was fine.

Late in the afternoon I asked again. However, this time he looked at me, shook his head, and said, "No, no, I'm not!" It broke my heart. Finally, the nurse came in with morphine to dull the pain. It took a while for his body to relax, but during those hours God gave us a gift I will never forget.

Because his appetite had diminished several weeks before, my stepmom and I often tried to think of things he would enjoy eating, perhaps pudding or ice cream. That afternoon, something came to mind — Dad loved watermelon!

Why neither of us thought of it before surprised us. When she mentioned watermelon to Dad at about four o'clock that afternoon, he perked up and said, "Yes."

"Sounds good. We will bring you some in the morning."

Just thirty minutes later a nurse brought his dinner tray. The three of us looked at the meal with amazement. On the tray was exactly what Dad had asked for — watermelon! He thoroughly enjoyed his treat, and we rejoiced in God's goodness to bring the very thing he wanted at precisely the right time. Surely, that menu had been decided by staff weeks before, but God knew on that day, for that meal, Dad would ask for watermelon.

He fell asleep shortly after dinner. The next morning, as I sat on the side of his bed singing hymns, he quietly, and ever so peacefully, passed from this life to the presence of his loving Savior.

That morning, Psalm 139:16 filled my heart. "All the days ordained for me were written in your book before one of them came to be." These words took on beautiful new meaning as God so wonderfully showed me that indeed each day—up to the very last—of my Dad's life had been written before he was born.

What a blessing that for his last meal here on earth I fed Dad spoonfuls of watermelon.

Linda Boyd's heart is to encourage others through her writing of God's faithfulness and goodness in both the sunshine and shadows of life. She recently completed her life-long goal of a college degree. Linda is the mother of two adult children, Lisa and David, and currently lives in Camarillo, California.

Mindy Ferguson

A Father's Love

ANSWERING PHONES IN my church office one cool December day, I received a call from a friend. After some casual bantering about our personal holiday plans and updates on our families, she told me about a young couple who recently had their first child. The young father and mother were struggling to earn enough money for their basic needs and didn't have any funds for Christmas gifts. The husband worked for an electrical contracting company during the day and his wife worked part-time in the evenings at a local department store. My concerned friend asked me if the church staff would be willing to organize an effort to provide Christmas dinner, some groceries, and a few gifts for the family. I told her I would make some phone calls and see what we could do.

After talking to the pastors, I called the young father. When I asked what his family needed, he simply replied, "We need a car seat and a safety gate for the baby." This young couple was struggling to buy groceries. Yet, the only requests the new daddy made were items necessary to keep his baby boy safe. I told him I would see what we could do and get back to him.

Within thirty minutes of that conversation, I received a call from another member of our church, informing me that her employer was interested in providing Christmas gifts for a needy family. Excited, I told her about the young couple and their baby's needs. She immediately agreed to provide the badly needed car seat and a safety gate. To my surprise, she also committed to providing diapers, baby formula, some clothing, and a few toys for the baby. I was overwhelmed by the goodness of God to provide even more than the humble father had requested.

With the baby's needs met, I sent an email to a few of the small group leaders from our church, letting them know about the family and suggesting they consider taking an offering to help provide groceries for the family. Within the hour, the members of one small group agreed to purchase a two-hundred dollar gift certificate to a local grocery store. A couple hours later, I received a call from a woman whose family was being transferred overseas. She had a freezer full of meat that she offered to donate to a needy family. I told her about the young couple and helped her set up a time to deliver the freezer—fully stocked with meat—to the young couple's home.

On Christmas Eve, I had the privilege of presenting the donated baby items and grocery store gift certificate to the family. The young father wept as he walked into the Sunday school room where we'd gathered all of the donated baby items. The room was filled with brightly wrapped packages for their boy. I handed him the grocery store gift certificate and said, "Jesus loves you." I too began to cry as I helped him load all of the packages into his truck.

My heart overflowed with love as I witnessed the humble request of a young, struggling father met by a lavish outpouring from His Heavenly Father.

Mindy Ferguson is a national speaker and Bible teacher. She is the author of *Walking with God: From Slavery to Freedom; Living the Promised Life* and *Hugs Bible Reflections for Women* and lives in Cypress, Texas with her husband of twenty-three years and their children. Visit her web site at www.FruitfulWord.org.

Amber Spriggs

Unbroken

EVERYDAY, IT'S WAR. Every morning, every dejected look in that mirror. Why can't I look like her? Why can't I change this haunting chorus of hate ringing in my ears? *You're fat; you have man arms,* says a raspy voice, *and if I were you, no one would ever see my feet.*

Fighting has become useless. "Why can't you love me," I cry. "Why can't you accept me?"

All I can do is stare at my face, that person I call a mistake—trying my best to make myself look beautiful, to be content with who I am.

"You are beautiful," a gentle Voice whispers. "You are perfect just the way you are. You are my lovely and perfect child. I love you."

"Then why can't I see it?" My tears well up. "Why can't I see my own beauty? Why can't I love myself?" I fall to my knees, hair masking my face, hands trembling at my eyes. "Why?"

Long moments of pain pass, then I stand once more and look at myself. *You're ugly, you're dumb, you're fat,* the raspy voice screams.

"No!" My heart pounds against my chest, and my hands shake. I throw my brush at the mirror, and it shatters into a million pieces. But the evil voice grows louder and louder, shouting *you're worthless, you're worthless.*

"Leave," shouts an authoritative voice.

In that moment, the screaming ends and my heartbeat slows. I cry in silence, thanking God for his ever-present and powerful authority over the cruel voice.

"You are beautiful," I hear the Voice again. "You are perfect just the way you are. You are my lovely and perfect child. I love you."

"Really God?" I say. "Then why do I hate myself?"

"Look," the Voice says.

I glance at the splintered mirror, and the broken pieces begin to place themselves together. Now I see my reflection smiling back at me, and I notice the glow in my eyes, the joy curving my lips, and the calmness of my being.

"You are beautiful. You are perfect just the way you are. You are my lovely and perfect child. I love you."

"God, is that you?" I cry in desperation.

Before I even know what is happening, my reflection nods and reaches through the mirror in an inviting way. I hesitate but know I must take its hand, so I reach.

My reflection blurs backward. The mirror consumes me.

Beep, beep, my alarm sounds. I open my eyes and realize I've been dreaming. Anxious, I run to the bathroom and find everything in its place—no broken glass. I look at the mirror and smile.

"You are beautiful. You are perfect just the way you are. You are my lovely and perfect child. I love you."

My heart sings, and my face brightens into a smile. I walk back to my room, grab my Bible, and open to 1 Corinthians 6:19: "Don't you know your body is the temple of the Holy Spirit who lives in you, and was given to you by God? You don't belong to yourself." Then I turn to Genesis 1:27: "So God created man in His own image; of God he created them; male and female He created them."

With tingly limbs, I look to heaven and whisper, "Lord, please help me, help me to love myself. To love who I am, and what I look like. Lord, please—I can't do this alone."

Amber Spriggs is 15 years old and lives in Albuquerque, New Mexico. She's adopted by Chad and Deanna Spriggs, has three siblings, and owns seven dogs. She started writing at 12 years of age and loves penning stories. She loves listening to music, hanging out with friends, and writing poetry.

Sherri Cullison

From Empty to Overflowing

MY CUP WAS empty. Hollow and hopeless, I longed for heaven. Months earlier, my youngest daughter Sarah, at the tender age of 14, took her own life. Day after day I dreaded each sunrise, because that meant I had to face another day. I missed my daughter, and fear gripped my weary mind. Every purpose in my life halted. My husband and I continued to cling to our faith, but there were moments in our weakness when we challenged God. I wrestled with darkness, and I wrestled with God.

The following year, my husband and I toured the Holy Land. We visited the Garden Tomb where Jesus was buried. As I walked into the garden, I felt like I had stepped out of Kansas into the wonderful Land of Oz. An array of beautiful trees and flowers surrounded the winding pathways. Sparrows chirping in the trees drowned annoying noises outside the holy walls. It soothed my soul. I took a deep breath, and closed my eyes to relish the moment. As I exhaled, I realized I had not been able to breathe that deeply for months.

We approached the tomb of Jesus and a cool breeze brushed my face and lifted my hair. It felt like a breath of fresh air entered my heart. God gave me CPR, reviving my soul. I walked through this magnificent garden of beauty, and a smile formed on my face. I felt at home. I stepped into my Savior's tomb and was convicted to examine my own sin. I wanted to mourn, but I couldn't. I remembered times following my little girl's death that I couldn't stop crying. Then there were times, for whatever reason, I couldn't cry at all. I thought to myself, "If I could cry now, surely healing would come." I reflected on the pain Jesus suffered on the cross for me. A tear rolled down my cheek. A spirit of worship grew in my heart, and I felt grateful. After another deep breath, I exhaled, easier still.

I looked down. Around my legs fluttered several pure white butterflies. They seemed playful like giggling children on a playground. Then I saw one bright yellow butterfly, different from all the rest. Sarah loved the color yellow, so when I saw the butterfly, I gasped. Could this be God telling us Sarah was with Him? After all, a butterfly is the symbol of new life. In a moment the darkness lifted. My empty cup filled with the comfort of God's love. My husband said, "Look, the white butterflies are like angels, and God is telling us Sarah is with Him." Heaviness lifted from my tired shoulders. The power of God's voice broke through my barriers of grief with butterflies, a gentle analogy of new life. I was amazed the Redeemer who died for all mankind revealed Himself to me in a moment of silent beauty. How appropriate He revealed that Sarah was precious enough to Him to save her soul, and I was precious enough for God to reveal that I was worth the extra effort. For the first time in a very long time, my spirit was overwhelmed with His unconditional love. A poem of praise became a moment of healing.

As I continued walking, the yellow butterfly followed me. I stopped; it stopped. I walked, and it fluttered beside me. I felt like a child again with a new imaginary friend, but this was very real, and very God. I wanted to tell everyone. I wanted to share it with the whole world. I wanted every soul to feel what I felt—wanted and loved. The wine of thankfulness overflowed the cup of my heart with a new-found hope. I closed my eyes, and whispered aloud, "Thank you, Lord." These words slipped across my lips like a secret between friends.

With every sunrise, I now know God's mercies are new every morning. My heart is satisfied to share the overflow of hope and new purpose I have found in Him.

Sherri Cullison is a writer living in Kingman, Arizona.

Suzy Haynes

The Deep Blue Unknown

Am I handling this? Or is it handling me?
I have my hands ready, just waiting to be set free.
Yet I am already free, just afraid to jump in,
Afraid to place my foot on the plank and walk to the edge.
I am not forced to or tied up.
Yet I am getting closer to that deep blue unknown
Where danger, adventure, uncertainty, and excitement await me.
What will I find?

It does not matter, as long as my eyes are on You, Lord.
You will reach down to the net that tries to entangle me.
You hold out Your hand to me.
Looking up to You gives me encouragement.
It restores hope in my heart, which supplies my soul,
And comes bubbling out of my mouth.
May my voice burst forth melodies of grace.

As I encounter each person, may Your Words be there,
Let not my selfishness take their place.
May my mouth be filled and overflowing with truth words,
May Your words supply honey to my tongue.
Lord, never take the words from me.

Suzy Haynes is from Colleyville, TX. Her passion for writing began when poetry became the only way for her feelings to make sense. Later a college project fueled her love for writing curriculum for young people. She has self-published three eight-week discipleship studies for teenagers.

Cindy Martin

Life Is Hard and God Is Good

HELLO, IT'S ME and it's time—I'm on the way to the hospital now. I will meet you there." The clock read 12:37 a.m. I had just nestled my head into the sweet spot of my pillow, weary from a day of Christmas celebrations complete with an abundance of food, family, and fun. My hand trembled as I hung up the phone. Any thought of anticipated slumber quickly evaporated as my head began to comprehend the magnitude of the words I had just heard. After several miscarriages, an unexplained diagnosis of infertility, and numerous failed adoption attempts, we were finally on our way to have a baby. Plans had been made for the arrival of our long awaited child to come in early January, but it was Christmas night and there was no waiting.

As we scrambled to get dressed a fresh wave of adrenalin hit and with lightning speed my husband backed the car out of the garage as I grabbed the packed diaper bag that poignantly held the hopes I had been carrying in my heart for years. Morning after morning, month after month, year after year, I had dreamed of this day.

We raced to the hospital with our hearts in a state of reckless abandon, pounding like marathon runners getting their first glimpse of the finish line. The realization of our dream was in sight, but all too soon it would fade into a nightmare. The woman who desired to gift us with our son suffered significant complications during delivery, and as a result both of their lives hung in the balance. They were each flown by medi-vac helicopters to larger hospitals in hopes their lives could be spared. My husband and I stood by the window, our noses pressed against the glass like forgotten puppies, watching in disbelief as the helicopter lifted off. Overcome by shock and looming devastation, I held onto the nearby railing as my knees no longer supported me. "God, why does it have to be so hard to have a baby?"

My heart churned as we drove to the hospital where the helicopter took our son, Randy. I was too overwhelmed to cry. My doer personality was powerless to do anything, and I sat in a heap, drowning in feelings of disbelief, betrayal by God, and hopelessness. Each mile we drove, my heart grew increasingly anxious as I wondered if Randy would still be alive when we got there. What if he's not? "God, You wouldn't allow that to happen to us after all we've been through, would You? I know life isn't supposed to be easy, but this is so hard. I don't know if I can do this. It wasn't supposed to happen this way."

As nervous tension accelerated through my body, I rocked back and forth, exasperated by my inability to fix the situation. I stared out the window of our car wondering if I was destined to travel down the road of empty arms once again.

"You know, God, this baby is Your child, You made him and it's *Your* job to take care of him." I scolded. God's reply was immediate.

"I *know* it's My job. Please let Me do it."

When I agreed with God that He had the right to orchestrate the events of my life, release replaced the panic and dread. The intensity of the situation still lingered, but the sense of despair melted away. God brought me hope that anchored my soul. Hope prevailed and our son (and his birth mother) survived. After many difficult days, we took our Christmas present home and began to "unwrap" him. In the months to come, he received a diagnosis of cerebral palsy.

I knew there would be many more difficult days ahead, but I also knew God would meet me in each of them and He has. I have experienced what it is like to be cared for by Almighty God in the midst of the storms of my life. I am no longer on the sidelines watching someone else. This is me, thrust onto center stage. Overwhelmed and vulnerable, I come to Him. And true to His Word, His grace is enough and His strength embraces my weakness. Indeed, life is hard and God is good, but you don't know how good God can be until you know how hard life can get.

Cindy and her husband of 21 years live with their two children near Calgary, Alberta, Canada. She is passionate about people experiencing the difference Jesus desires to make in their everyday lives. She shares this passion as a writer and speaker. Visit www.lifemeetsreality.com for more information.

Judy McLaughlin

THE OLD GRAY MARE

SERVING THE LORD has always been an important part of living for me. I never thought the day would come that I outlived my usefulness to the Lord. But it did. Let's just say that I didn't do well with arriving at the age of maturity. I felt like an old gray mare—over-the-hill, useless, done. I was downright low.

One morning as I sat contemplating with the Lord, I began to enter into what seemed to be an out of body experience, high and lifted up. I walked alongside the Lord Jesus as He explained to me that I had not yet come to the end of my journey. He confirmed the path he established for me, the one He Himself structured. He instructed me to continue walking it. I still had work to do for His kingdom.

The Lord and I spent the day together, enjoying each other's company and conversation. I was in awe, though apparently, not speechless.

To be honest, I can't say much more than that. I don't remember the conversation or even what I saw, only the blips I already shared. But I do remember the sense of peace that came upon me. It filled me with an overwhelming warmth. Joy! Elation!

While only a vision, this experience changed my life. The memory of it still overcomes me with a sense of peace and the presence of the Holy Spirit.

Now I can't wait to get away with the Lord every day for devotions, readings, and prayers. In our special times together He gives me wisdom and knowledge for the upcoming day. I can let go of worry and face the world with a bounce in my step, knowing I please the Father. I can just be myself. When He says that He calls you by name and you were created for His pleasure, He truly means it.

I am able to accomplish things that a few months before would have seemed impossible. No longer "the old gray mare," my energy, health, and stamina reach beyond understanding. As a volunteer, I give of myself completely, mentally and physically. I keep a clean house, cook three meals a day, host a ladies Bible study and still have time for my favorite refreshment, grocery shopping. Put me in a Costco or Sam's, and I will peruse the aisles for hours.

I am experiencing renewed passion to be who God made me to be. From attending Women of Destiny to working at the CLASS Christian Writers Conference where I serve as the conference administrator, God continues to expand my ministry opportunities. Not to brag about my accomplishments, but to give glory to God for allowing me to see into His kingdom and share His love with people around me.

One of my lifelong friends recently became very ill, requiring her to move to a facility for assisted living. I am now able to be a caregiver to her in a way that I never could have before my encounter with the Lord. She's confined to a wheelchair, but I take her out once a week for lunch. Then we get our nails and hair done. What a time we have, laughing and remembering the good old days, when she's alert enough to remember. My heart sometime breaks. But I wouldn't exchange those outings for anything in the world.

During one of those outings, I asked her if she wanted to know Jesus. She responded with a "yes," and I got to lead my sweet friend to the Lord. My God is awesome!

Over the past months, I've found out that I have a job to complete for the Lord. I can share my experiences, my talents, and my prayers with whomever God brings across my path. I am no old gray mare. I am a valuable, vibrant woman of God, a daughter of the King. He calls me by name and uses me to expand His kingdom.

You, too, have been called. No matter your age or status, the Lord wants to use you. Call out His name, Jesus. He will respond. Maybe He'll invite you for a walk where you can enjoy an amazing conversation.

Judy McLaughlin is a Bible study leader and Certified Personality Trainer. When not volunteering in one of many activities at her church in Albuquerque, she can be found working behind the scenes for CLASSEMINARS or winning bowling tournaments. Married to Jerry for 53 years, they have one daughter, Gayleen. Judy loves to encourage others in their walks with the Lord.

Rick Steele

My Most Memorable Christmas

I HAVE HAD a lot of memorable Christmases in the forty-one years God has given me so far. Forgive me for saying this, but Christmas is not my favorite time of year. In fact, my wife will be the first to tell you I am a scrooge. Now that we have a son, I admit I enjoy the holiday season a bit more when I see the joy and sparkle in his eyes as the anticipation of opening presents builds. Nevertheless, the stress that comes with juggling work responsibilities along with preparing for the festivities of December 25th can bring out the worst in me and other family members. Plus the approach of Christmas reminds me that yet another year is almost over, and I regret not accomplishing the things I wanted to. At the very least the Christmas season makes me yearn for December 26th and the clean slate of a new year.

But then I am reminded of Christmases during simpler times when I was young. I remember having the same anticipation my son experiences today. I remember the magical Christmases of the 1970s and 80s and the closeness of family. One particular Christmas is seared in my memory—Christmas, 1981.

I was in seventh grade, and times were very tough for my family. My father has been a pastor most of my life, but this particular year he was forced out of his position with a small congregation in rural southern Ohio. I was the oldest of five children at that time. (Two more sisters would come later.) Dad was forced to go on unemployment benefits and began looking for any type of work to support the family. But this was in the middle of a hard-hitting recession in the early Reagan years, one especially felt in the rustbelt state of Ohio and the Appalachian region we lived in. Jobs were scarce. He and Mom warned us there would be no Christmas presents under the tree this year, and we older kids knew they were dead serious this time.

Christmas Eve came and went. It was a normal Christmas Eve; one marked by third-tier college bowl games and Bob Hope specials on TV. Then bedtime came. Everyone in the household had gone to sleep. Around 1 a.m., we were awakened by the blaring sounds of a car horn. I looked out of my upstairs bedroom window and saw two women dressed in Santa outfits get out of the car. My startled parents came to the door to see what was going on. The lady Santas then proceeded to take one wrapped present after another out of their vehicle. Then they marched the presents into our house and placed them under our Christmas tree. I can remember hearing my father tell the Santas that there must have been some mistake.

"No mistake," they exclaimed.

"Are you sure you came to the right place?"

"Yes, we are sure."

"Well, who sent you here then?" Dad asked.

"God sent us," was the quick, matter-of-fact reply.

"How can we thank you?" Dad asked a final time.

"Thank the Lord for his goodness," said the ladies as they got back in their vehicle and drove off into the night.

To this day, none of the family know who those women were. I sometimes like to think they were real angels sent from God. The presents they brought us that night were not the most awe-inspiring presents we ever received, but they made that Christmas extra special. It was a time when God poured out blessings of mercy to a family that needed it more than any other time. As an adult, when I get crotchety about the hustle and bustle of Christmas and all of its pressures, the thoughts of that Christmas in 1981 put things in proper perspective for me.

We often describe that Christmas as miraculous. Maybe it was or wasn't, but it always gets me to thinking of that first Christmas that no doubt was miraculous. A time when God sent his one and only Son to come to earth to be born to an ordinary teenage peasant girl. Thinking of this greatest gift to mankind makes me appreciate the true reason for the season, and suddenly this old scrooge gets a little Christmas spirit. Thank God for the greatest Christmas gift and for memories of simpler times!

Rick Steele is an accomplished writer/editor who has managed the workflow of over 100 titles for AMG Publishers in Chattanooga, TN. Rick has been at the forefront of AMG's growing list of Bible study products. He and his family enjoy their Christmases near Georgia.

Gloria Penwell

But Mom, That's My Miracle

AFTER LIVING IN a house full of guys, I was thrilled when a baby girl named Darcey joined our family.

When she was born she had an angry looking red birthmark on her arm. The doctor told us it would fade with time and not be as noticeable. We took her home, but the birthmark did not fade. In fact, it got redder and began to feel feverish. Each time we took her to see the doctor he told us the same thing. "Be patient, it will get better."

Soon the birthmark became infected. Keeping it clean and covered was hard with a small baby. The doctor was now perplexed. He had never seen this happen before. As weeks passed the wound got uglier and uglier. Finally, the doctor sent us to a pediatric specialist.

The specialist told us that unless the birthmark began to heal in two months he would have to do surgery. At that point Darcey was six months old. The specialist was hesitant to do the operation because there would be many blood vessels involved. There was the very real danger she could bleed to death.

We walked out of the doctor's office in stunned silence. Our only thought was that we must call our friends and family and beg them to pray. Soon the phone was ringing incessantly with well-wishes and promises for prayer. People from all over the states and several foreign countries were lifting up our precious little girl before the Father.

One day our son, Daren, who was three at the time, was playing with Darcey on the floor in the living room. I was in the kitchen making dinner when I heard a horrible noise. Both Daren and Darcey were crying at the top of their lungs.

I ran into the room to see Daren laying beside Darcey on the rug. He was sobbing, "Mommy, I didn't mean to hurt her boo-boo." He had rolled over her while they were playing and knocked the scab off of her wound. For a few minutes panic reigned until I was able to clean up Darcey's sore, and then convince Daren that sissy was going to be all right.

As the days went by the birthmark began to heal. By the time we took her back to the specialist it was nearly healed over. The doctor told us that, to his amazement, there wouldn't be any need for the surgery. Praise God. All those prayers raised up for our daughter had been answered.

As she got older one of our friends upon seeing her always said, "Show me your miracle." She would hold up her arm with great pride to show him.

When Darcey was going into high school Dan and I told her we would be happy to have the scar that covered the birthmark removed. Her reply to me was, "But Mom, that's my miracle." How do you argue with that?

Gloria Penwell has traveled to many Christian writers conferences with her late husband Dan Penwell editor at AMG Publishers. She has a love for writers and endeavors to encourage new writers. She was honored to assist in the 2010 Class Christian Writers Conference.

Larry C. Davis

Life Is Precious

JANUARY 16, 2011, MY HIGH school sweetheart and I will celebrate forty years of marriage where we have witnessed God's grace and overflow in our lives. Early in our marriage, I became an embalmer and have since worked in the funeral profession for thirty-eight years. However, I am getting ahead of myself.

On December 17, 1969, I had agreed to play Santa for a four-year old friend of Linda's. Our little friend, Gina, was quite impressed with my rendition of Santa. I was dressed in a red velvet suit trimmed in white fur with a large pillow and a fake beard. I had pulled it off; Gina was happy and Linda was grateful, and we were off to my mother's house to change clothes and head out for dinner.

Linda was driving my 1964 red Malibu because I was still dressed as Santa, pillow and all. As we approached my mother's home, Linda complained of a headache. Little did we know that our lives were about to change, forever. While I was changing from Santa to Larry I heard my mother's scream. Linda was lying on the entry floor in convulsions and holding her head in pain. I was terrified.

Following a month in the hospital, Linda was diagnosed with Ateriovascular Malformation (AVM), a knot of blood vessels which serve no purpose. Her AVM is a birth defect found most often during certain autopsies when people die in their seventies or eighties. God was very present and so good during this most difficult time. He provided for a wonderful Christian neurosurgeon who advised Linda and her parents that the AVM was dangerously close to the brain stem and could not be removed. Following several months of recovery Linda returned to a normal lifestyle with few restrictions.

We were young and in love; the concerns of AVM seemed to diminish with time and within months we were talking marriage. Our parents and friends encouraged us in our wedding plans. Perhaps because they feared another bleed could end Linda's life, and they wanted as much happiness for us as possible. On Saturday, January 16, 1971, when we were nineteen years old, we were married.

While attending college and working part-time as a florist I attended a Methodist Men's steak dinner featuring a speaker from Draper Mortuary. I was intrigued while the speaker told of his ministry as a funeral professional. The ministry aspect of serving people during the most difficult days of their lives, moved me. I became an apprentice embalmer and began my ministry of serving families.

As years went by, Linda's AVM became dormant, however not forgotten. Linda suspected that she may be expecting a baby during our second year of marriage. While her doctors had warned us of the risks and poor prospects of a successful pregnancy with an AVM, they confirmed we were expecting. During this time I was attending Mortuary College learning my craft and dealing with the realities of death, everyday. I could not help thinking about the knot of vessels surging with blood in the base of my wife's brain. Although the risks of Linda's death during childbirth were extreme, on Valentine's Day, 1974, we shared the greatest treasure yet from God—the birth of our son, Douglas. We were overflowing with praise and thanksgiving! We had made it through, and the doctors insisted we fix things so none of us were put through the challenge of pregnancy again. God's overflow continues in our lives. Douglas is now a thirty-six year old architect living a wonderful Christian life.

Our journey has had many of the ups and downs most marriages experience. With my ministry in the funeral profession, I continue to appreciate every day of life. After all, any day above ground is a good day. Thirty-nine years after her first bleed and while on a relaxing vacation in Colorado, Linda's AVM bled. Following a week in ICU we returned to our home and resumed our lives in Indio, CA.

As of today, Linda has survived yet another bleed. Early in 2010, eighteen months after her last episode, the day after our thirty-ninth wedding anniversary, we were on our way to ER. God has restored Linda to good health. Our faith and my ministry have given us good reason to appreciate every day of life. God has a purpose, and we live with overflowing hearts full of gratitude.

Larry C. Davis is Vice President of Forest Lawn Memorial-Parks & Mortuaries in Palm Springs, Cathedral City, Indio, and Coachella, CA with thirty-eight years in the funeral profession. He was the founding director of Crystal Cathedral Memorial Gardens in Garden Grove, CA. He has spoken to churches, professional groups, high schools, and colleges.

Lindy Abbott

Do You Know My Father?

I SURVIVED HURRICANES, tornados, floods, and endless storms. As a child I thought some dark rainy days would never end. Suffocated by fear, hate, abuse, and trauma, too immense for words to speak, I wrote. Out of my heart flowed tears of pain, grief, loss, and shame. I wrote poems, songs, and stories that were simply rambling words pouring out, releasing my heart of its captivity. And for a short time, ever so brief, I felt as though I could breath.

I don't want to introduce you to my earthly father. To me, he is my source of all the agony I have suffered. I would never want someone to have to know him, to be hurt by him. No child deserves an abusive father, but the truth is many people know my father. They have been hurt beyond measure in unspeakable ways. Raped, beaten, starved, cursed, and spit upon. What child deserves a life like that?

Praise God, my life story doesn't end at the bottom of the miry pit: bruised, torn, and left for dead. Full of venom; hope for life was buried deep within. I want to tell you about Papa, My Father God. He is my Daddy, the only real Father I will ever have. He is more than enough. For me, my cup is full and runs over with His love.

How can one ever explain how God rescues His daughter from drowning in a well of despair, weighted down by bitterness, hatred, and regret? How can mere words ever grant the love of my Father's justice? They cannot, but His words can!

> "In the beginning was the Word and the Word was with God and the Word was God, and the Word was God. He was in the beginning with God. All things were made through Him, and without Him nothing was made that was made… in Him was life, and the life was the light of all men. And the light shines into the darkness."
>
> —John 1:51 (NKJV)

Today, I speak words, when and where God says. If the words were my own, they would be useless rubble tossed away as crumbled junk mail. God cannot be bought, nor can His words. His message is not for sale. He freely gives, so as a minister for my Lord I freely give words. Truly, the words are His to begin with and will never be my own to claim. My life story is His story of love, redemption, and grace. Apart from Him, I have nothing to say.

Without Him, I would still be drowning in the bottom of the well. Crying out, begging, "Please don't leave me. Please someone help me. I am frightened. I am lonely. I can't get out." God reached down and pulled me out of the miry pit, He rescued my soul when I had not yet known Him. He saved me from all of my sins before the day I was born. He is my Redeemer, my Savior, my Rescuer, my Lover, my Healer, my Father, my God! Who else could I have turned to? Who else would have stopped, moved by compassion to look at me, deep within my broken heart and know how to bind me up so that I could heal?

His timing is perfect. He is personal, intimate. He continues to heal me, to be who He originally created me to be. Don't you want to know My Father? He is safe, holy, knowing, loving, and beautiful. And humbly, in awe I say, "He is mine. He is my daddy. I belong to Him. I am His forever."

I am no longer the frightened, child of sorrow, I once was. God has made me new. The child, that could not find the words to express the unspeakable trauma of her soul, is spiritually reborn. I am my Father's daughter, and He gives me the words to bring Him glory. God is always with me, so out of my heart His message overflows to others wherever I go.

Lindy Abbott, a veteran homeschool mom, has a BA in Education. She is an experienced teacher, writer, and speaker. Lindy writes for www.takerootandwrite.com, is copy editor of Rooted Living e-magazine, and publishes several articles weekly. Lindy's ministry is helping hurting people, raising a godly heritage, and restoring God and Country. http://www.facebook.com/lindylou.abbott.

Sharon Baijense

GOD GAVE ME JOY

YOUR HEART CHANGES the moment you become a mom. It no longer belongs to you but to your family. It's the same with God. When we enter into a relationship with Him our heart undergoes a major change. It no longer belongs to you but to God. He loves it when we share our relationships, goals, dreams, and desires. I came to understand this through my own special Joy.

It was the typical laundry day when my six-year-old daughter Joy burst through the door. She paused and flashed her big brown eyes my direction. Seeing her impish smile grow and her eyes sparkle, I wondered what trouble she had gotten herself into. In all her joyfulness she giggled out almost as one word, "Mommy-I-love-you-you-have-beautiful-eyes." While smiling she took small steps forward and then quick steps back to run away. In an instant she was gone.

My heart was filled with emotion—surprise, joy, excitement, and love. I looked up to God and thanked Him for this wonderful little person in my life. Thinking about this fills my mind with thanks and praise to my Heavenly Father who gave me my children. In many ways, it is also a reminder to me of how God appreciates moments like these. Jesus said, "I tell you the truth, unless you change and become like little children, you will never enter the kingdom of heaven" (Matthew 28:3). We need to approach Him with a childlike heart, fully trusting, and with joy, always thankful He is our Father.

There is a reason why the Bible says, "Be thankful, always." God loves to hear little words like this from His children. In many ways it is like my little Joy. She knows she is loved, and when her heart bubbles over to express this in a spontaneous and childlike manner, my heart fills with joy as well. This makes me want to tip-toe up to my Heavenly Father, full of mischief and joy, and giggle," Father-I-Love-You-You-Have-Beautiful-Eyes."

Sharon Baijense has a heart for women struggling with weight loss. She knows the pain and discouragement of this battle through personal experience. She's a dynamic speaker full of humor and honest truth. Sharon gives women guidance and direction to succeed through discipline and lifestyle change. Contact Sharon at hsbaijense@aol.com

Lauren Parker

HURRICANE

THOUGHTS FADE. COLD disappears. Heat transmits through the bones. Emotion pours out of fingertips. Necks arch. Eyes lift.

In a moment, time stops.

The night glistens across the water toward the light spectacle—the space shuttle—shining in the blackened 4 a.m. dawn. Standing on the damp grass in icy February wind, people gaze, all waiting, all watching with anticipation, looking for even a movement from the towering machine.

Silence, silence, silence. It screams into the faces of the spectators who have traveled for many a night to witness the glory of humanity, the passion of hard work, and the superiority of mankind. Man, who is like him? He is the grandest thought of all. The silence screams of that. It screams of man's accomplishments, man's power, man's authority. Racing across the façade of the water, it screams and screams toward the metallic trophy, the ubiquitous rays proclaiming its might. Oh gaze at it all people! Gaze at what your hands have created! Gaze at what you have brought into existence!

"Two, one, zero, booster ignition," booms the voice from the loudspeakers. "And liftoff of Shuttle Endeavor!"

A low rumble grows into violent shaking. With a flash and the halting of time, the grand machine thrusts from the plume of fire and smoke into the dark sky. It paints a blue background, reveals the outline of the clouds, and causes the cold night to wish of noontide.

Breaths are held.

Suddenly time crashes back to reality as the space shuttle races through the air. Upward, upward it flies beyond the clouds and into the starscapes. Blue lights twinkle in excitement. Stars open their arms in joyful homecoming. Prayers lift upon the cold morning's breeze. Smaller the shuttle becomes—becomes a star, becomes creation.

The fire and smoke fade from reality and into the heart. All onlookers release their breaths as the sky returns to night. What is this magnificence? The screaming silence is hushed while watching the glorious space shuttle disappear against the bright lights. Oh the stars twinkle greater than man-made machines. The planets, but flecks of dust to the eye, are bigger than imagination can fathom. They hang upon nothing, invisible threads gliding them methodically throughout the empty. Whether or not the spectators can gaze into the outermost reaches of space, they begin to see colors explode and gases collide, trails of ice racing against light, dust and debris swirling about, waltzing with their celestial partners. Universes breathe in and breathe out, circling upon each other.

Oh where is the grand space shuttle? It is hidden among the grandeur of the cosmos, the beauty of the galaxies, the glory of God. The invisible hand of the Creator moves the threads, commands the spinning planets, describes the power of the black hole, fashions the delicate detail of the aurora borealis and the storms upon Jupiter. His hands guide the comets around their circuit; He orchestrates the song of the stars. He brought it all into existence. The galaxies laugh.

Oh what is that space shuttle? It is nothing.

Oh who is the astronaut? He is more. Above all created things, above the spinning planets and glistening stars and curtains of light, man is greater than them all. He is the height of God's creation, and more beautiful than the far reaches of space and the towering mountains of distant planets. And though man is great, God is infinitely greater, for when man is described as beautiful, God is the very essence of beauty. When man loves, God is love. The Lord is every good thing. He is beyond and before and above all knowledge and wisdom. He is the very Designer of the smallest cell and the largest galaxy. He is the One who calls man good and loves him unconditionally. No one dares imagine the majesty of God—for it is impossible.

Oh what is the space shuttle? It is nothing. It is nothing compared to the Creator of time. It is infinitely nothing and God is infinitely everything. It is a hill, while He a mountain. It is a stream, while He the ocean.

It is the trickle, while He a hurricane.

Lauren Parker is a 16-year-old writer who resides in Anchorage, Alaska, with her parents, three siblings, a crazy dog, and a psychotic cat. When not running in the snow in a T-shirt or attempting to stop her hiccup problem, Lauren enjoys photography and pretending to be a spy. Her blog is: impulsing.tumblr.com.

Pat Domangue

Waves of Mercy and Grace

"The Lord is gracious and full of compassion, slow to anger and great in mercy."
—Psalm 145:8

THE VACATION BIBLE School director told the twenty-two second graders to think of themselves like the toy Volkswagen she held. "You can use the church as a parking lot or a filling station." A small tan hand waved in the air and a little girl with chestnut-colored hair and big brown eyes said, "Sometimes bad things happen to me." She told about her mother's fight with her boyfriend and how she and her mother had been kicked out of their house. She said she could not see her daddy and wished she could.

As a volunteer I stood in the strained silence. My emotions were intense and my heart was torn. I was angry at the mother and upset with Jesus. "How could You? Why would You sit back and let this little one hurt?" Memories flashed through my mind of painful moments my child experienced before I knew the Lord. The Holy Spirit reminded me of the song we had sung in the VBS opening assembly about waves of mercy and waves of grace. Just a few years earlier I had been the recipient of His mercy and grace. This mother could have been me. Jesus was the one distinction between us. What if He had not been patient and long-suffering with me?

I remembered Jesus' disciples, James and John. In Luke 9:51-56 Jesus entered a Samaritan village and the people rejected Him. James and John were indignant. They wanted to rain down fire from heaven and consume them as Elijah did. Jesus responded, "You do not know what manner of spirit you are of. For the Son of Man did not come to destroy lives but to save them." I am thankful for these stories, exposing our weaknesses and flaws no matter how closely we may walk with Christ. Just a few verses back in the same chapter James and John had been with Jesus when He was transfigured on the mount. All the more reason they were so indignant. They had seen and experienced something others had not and thought everyone should receive Him as they did. Similar to how I felt that day; I knew Jesus and had experienced Him in extraordinary ways. Like James and John, my first instinct was to be angry and indignant with someone who did not know the Lord like I knew Him.

James and John's faith was strong. They believed they had the power and ability to call down fire from heaven. When we get mad and indignant we can get pretty bold. I wonder if the Lord is careful giving out His power because He knows we can be dangerous. Love and self-control are vital if we are to be trusted with His power. Jesus said, "You do not know what manner of spirit you are of," but He did. In Luke 6:45, He says "A good man out of the good treasure of his heart brings forth good; and an evil man out of the evil treasure of his heart brings forth evil. For out of the abundance of the heart his mouth speaks." What dangerous ground we tread calling down fire.

Jesus came to save not destroy. The word *save*, as used in Luke 9:56 is *sozo* in Greek and means to keep safe and sound, to rescue from danger or destruction. Do you see the opposing intentions of Jesus and His disciples? Can you relate to wanting to call down fire on someone who doesn't get it? What about waves of mercy and grace? We should call down the fire of the Holy Spirit who can ignite and engulf the heart with love for God and others. This fire can change the world and unjust circumstances. Spend a few minutes reflecting on a time that you deserved His holy fire to come down and consume you but instead you experienced the heart of a Savior who washed you in waves of mercy and grace.

Pat Domangue is the founder of On Fire Ministries, a ministry for women and teen girls, which is the parent ministry to "Girlfriends," a Christian women's talk show seen on Legacy TV. Pat is co-host of "Girlfriends" and a Bible study author. She is a wife and mother of three daughters.

Connie Payne

My Island of Refuge

HAVE YOU EVER received a gift that you had no idea you needed? That happened to me seventeen years ago. It was just an ordinary item, really—something I considered a comfortable convenience, yet not anything I'd spend much time thinking about. It turns out that God knew I needed this gift long before I did.

What's amazing is that—like a chameleon—it became what I needed most at that given time. Now, you might wonder how an ordinary object could do this, but God in His infinite wisdom took a commonplace gift and used it to bless my life over and over again.

Of all the possible things it could be, believe it or not—it was a bed. And not just any bed, but a king-size take-up-your-whole-room kind of bed. My parents were downsizing to a smaller home and no longer had space, so I became the obvious heir since my family was quickly expanding.

The first time I lay on this bed, I felt small. Here was this huge island, and I was the only inhabitant. With six children in the house, I had no idea that this island would become a refuge against the waves of the day.

My children soon realized that if they wanted my undivided attention, they could come into my room, flop on the bed, and share the events of their day. Before long, their routine chats turned into meaningful dialogue. Everything was shared—nothing was off-limits. My bed was an epicenter and conversation seemed to flow.

As the years passed, this sharing of life continued. I remember when my oldest son came in and fell onto my bed devastated by lost love. More than a few tears were shed that night. Six months later, that same son flopped on the bed and poured out his heart about his new love, the girl of his dreams who would later become his wife. Then came the day my younger son dropped in to talk about his homework—or so he thought. Without warning, his unconfessed sin came gushing out with the tears that had been stopped up for days. Thank goodness I had a top sheet. That night my bed became a confessional, and forgiveness was given and received by a hurting soul.

An island. A refuge. An epicenter. A sponge. A confessional. What more could my bed be? It would soon let me know.

While my husband and I were attending the funeral of a long-time family friend, we received a phone call. My dad was crying. Through painful sobs, he gave the news of Mom's cancer. "Things look bad," he said, but all I could hear was the rushing of wind, something about tests, the hospital… I don't know. My life stood still.

A year after Mom was gone, Dad called with the news of his own cancer. I was still worn out from taking care of Mom, but God gave me the strength to care for Dad, too. There was joy amidst the pain of ushering my parents to the next life, but I was left totally exhausted—inside and out.

My bed was waiting, so afterward I went home and put life on hold. I did nothing outside of work for two whole years. I didn't even go to church. In the comfort of my bed, I prayed to God and studied his Word. He reached down and healed my heart with a peace I had never known before. In the quiet calm of that bed, I received exactly what I needed.

Life continues, and I have never been more renewed. The love, joy, and peace coming out of that simple, ordinary bed keep overflowing. My oldest daughter just came in and plopped down my eleven-month old grandbaby. We all lie on the bed and talk about the new little sister due in a few months.

It's hard for me to imagine life without this big bed now. The blessings keep on coming.

Connie Payne and her husband, Scott, have worked with the homeless at Inner City Mission in Springfield, Illinois for the past sixteen years. Connie hopes to write on homeless issues and Christian living. She has six children and a granddaughter. Connie can be contacted at: connie@innercitymission.net.

Marilyn Stewart

THE LIGHT FROM OUTSIDE

MY FAVORITE PICTURE of the damage left by Hurricane Katrina—if it's possible to have a favorite picture of a disaster—was taken in the sanctuary of my church after it filled with nine feet of water when the nearby levee broke in the storm's aftermath.

At first glance, the picture doesn't make sense. There is a spot in the corner that seems out of place. Receding water left the sanctuary filled with rancid mud and piles of moldy debris. The dim background of the picture shows one end of a long pew resting on the rusted strings of the baby-grand piano. The piano lid stands rusted in place behind it, pushed open by moving water. But the pure-white spot in the corner is so bright it almost dazzles. Flowing around the spot are brilliant streaks of turquoise-blue.

What the camera lens didn't show was that light was streaming in from outside through a broken stained glass window and falling onto the corner like a spotlight. Under the brilliant light, the corner looked as if it had been scrubbed clean. The photo is my favorite because it tells my story of the storm.

A year after the photo was taken, my family returned to New Orleans where mail delivery was sporadic and doctors hard to find. For my children, the storm meant the loss of a year of high school sports and a chance at certain scholarships. Every day chores like buying groceries took from the precious little time I had for writing, and I chaffed when I thought that God had led us back.

Like the unexpected light in the dark room, God was working in my life when I didn't know it. An email one day brought an opportunity to cover the stories of the volunteers from around the nation who came to the aid of our city. The volunteers often cried as they told of finding a husband's ring in the rubble and returning it to his widow, or salvaging a homemade bookcase signed, "Love, Daddy." I walked away in tears, shamed that strangers loved my city more than I did.

Only months earlier, I had questioned why God would bring us to a place so broken. The volunteers' overflowing love for those in need was one of the things God used to show me He is not content to let me live out an empty life focused on myself. Slowly, gratitude began to warm my heart and I found it was easier to accept the shortcomings and failures of others. I found a fresh passion for sharing the Gospel even in the French Quarter and a new willingness to love and accept others as they were. I am learning that God's answers come in unexpected ways. When we commit all to Him, He gives back to us in abundance what we really needed all along. We need him.

I often stumble and am called again to give my dreams, my children, and my writing completely over to God. But I wouldn't go back to who I was before the storm, even if I could. Though I still have far to go, I see how far I've come.

Sometimes when I walk through the sanctuary alone, with only the low afternoon sun to light the room, I remember the picture and smile. And I am grateful and amazed.

Marilyn J. Stewart writes features and a weekly column as a contributing writer to *The Times-Picayune* of New Orleans. She also writes for *The Baptist Message*, the newsjournal of Louisiana Southern Baptists, and her articles have appeared on Baptist Press and in numerous state Baptist newspapers.

Glenda Durano

It's All Good

I REMEMBER BEING completely befuddled in sixth grade when I discovered that I could not "be good." In the basement of my junior high school, Mrs. Hornbeck, our English teacher, enlightened us, "When someone enquires 'How are you?' the proper response is either 'I'm doing fine' or 'I'm doing well.' One should never respond, 'I'm fine,' and certainly not, 'I'm good.'" She voiced the latter with such disdain that I immediately knew this transgression was tantamount to breaking one of the Ten Commandments.

The grammar lesson that day had something to do with adverbs and predicate adjectives, and it was all very confusing. To be honest, I'm still not sure that I completely understand what Mrs. Hornbeck was attempting to teach.

Today, when junior high students are asked, "How are you?" they answer, "Awesome," or even more frequently, "It's all good." Poor Mrs. Hornbeck would roll over in her grave! The fact of the matter, however, is that it *is* all good—at least, according to Romans 8:28, it is: "And we know that in all things, God works for the good of those who love Him, who have been called according to His purpose" (NIV).

The problem arises, however, when our definition of good and God's definition of good do not match. We tend to determine our degree of good based on our circumstances instead of our salvation, often giving way to situational faith.

I have to admit that I've had a blessed life, and, until a few years ago, I was quite satisfied with God's good because His definition matched mine very well. My husband was the top luxury green builder in the nation; my children attended a private university on scholarship; we lived in a million-dollar-plus home; we even ministered to those less fortunate. Life, overall, *was* good. Until 2008.

My husband blamed our sudden negative turn of fortune on his poor business decisions, but to me it seemed as if God was simply calling our names. Our savings plummeted; our investments were in non-income producing dirt; and we were staring foreclosure in the face. At one point, my husband sat down with me at the kitchen table and proposed that we simply walk away from our home and its $5,000-a-month mortgage. I convinced him not to, first, because we had a financial obligation to the bank and, secondly, I believed that if we walked away from this lesson, we'd eventually have to learn it again. Our identity had become tied to our situation rather than our salvation, and this was a lesson worth learning. Unlike Mrs. Hornbeck, God never allows His instruction to go unlearned. We never fail His class. Instead, we just take it over and over, until one day, the proverbial two-by-four hits us in the head and we "get it."

This time, however, just when I thought I was beginning to "get it," God saved me missing the point—again. While taking a discipleship class at church, I had to memorize Romans 8:28-29. *Piece of cake*, I thought to myself, since Romans 8:28 had always been one of my favorite scriptures. I scribbled the familiar Romans 8:28 on my memory card, but as I wrote down verse 29, it hit me as never before: "For those God foreknew, He also predestined to be conformed to the likeness of His Son that He might be the firstborn among many brothers." Conformed to the likeness of His Son—that was "the good" of Romans 8:28. Not money. Not situations. Not physical blessings. But conformity to Him.

While our situation today remains basically the same, my husband and I are slowly learning to accept and even value God's definition of good. We're trying to see things from His eternal perspective. Too many times, we base our faith on the facts—things we can see and feel—the situation—instead of basing our faith on the truth that God loves us and will do whatever it takes to conform us to His likeness.

Therefore, today, when people ask me "How are you?" I knowingly respond—with apologies to Mrs. Hornbeck—"It's all good"—because *it is*!

As an independent education consultant, Glenda Durano coaches teenagers in discovering their passions, developing their potential, and determining the path that God has for them, particularly with regard to college. Active in ministry for over 30 years, she loves helping others find their niche. www.competitivecollegecoaching.com.

Aaron M. Zook, Jr.

God's in Charge; Enjoy the Ride

THE COOL MORNING air carried the strong scent of spruce trees. Shafts of light yellow came through our vinyl window, speckling part of our camping gear inside the cramped six-man tent. I rolled onto my left side to rub my eyes.

I glanced at my watch. Six-thirty: wake-up time. I nudged my wife, who shifted to another comfortable position without waking. Using great stealth, I snuck out of the sleeping bag, dressed in a swimsuit, T-shirt and sandals, then slipped past our 11- and 13- year-old sleeping boys. The morning mist brushed my face as I emerged like a sleepy bear, stretching my six-foot frame in a silent yawn.

Dancing flames from the newly lit campfire warmed my fingers. Clinking camp-stove pots and pans punctuated nature's quiet while I prepared to cook scrambled eggs, bacon, and hot water for tea.

Joyce popped her head out of our tent, smiling. "When's breakfast?"

"Thirty minutes, hon."

"OK, I'll get the boys ready." She disappeared.

Eventually, Jeremiah and Mike burst through the zippered door, ready to eat. Joyce followed, giving me a light kiss.

"What a beautiful day," she said.

Golden rays accentuated the rich fall colors of the cherry, elm, birch, and sumac trees in the Chain O'Lakes wilderness camping area. The temperature was perfect. After we thanked the Lord for His provision, we ate breakfast. Campsite clean-up was next, followed by packing a lunch, storing food, and taking a short hike around the campgrounds. We strolled into the boat rental office by ten o'clock.

"Two canoes, please," I requested.

The young clerk smiled. "No problem," He handed us our paddles and recited mandatory safety instructions.

"Can we get to all eight lakes?" Mike bluntly asked.

"Sorry," the clerk said. "The water level is down, so you can't reach all eight." The clerk gave us a map, highlighting available lakes. "This is Sand Lake. Three connected lakes are to the right and four are to the left."

Unhappy, Mike's head hung down and his springy walk turned into a shuffle. Jeremiah's face frowned. Our goal of visiting all eight lakes was dashed. However, seeing the canoes at the dock changed their disillusionment to excitement.

"I'm with Dad!" Jeremiah cried out.

"Not so fast," I said. "You two boys go together first. Stay within shouting distance. You're our scouts."

"OK," Jeremiah and Michael both replied.

We raced canoes to get across Sand Lake. In ten minutes, we were all worn out!

"Slow down a little," I said. "Go left."

The canoes rocked gently as we paddled. Gliding near the shore, we pointed out white-tailed deer, rabbits, and chipmunks. We navigated the first canal to Weber Lake, which we named the Lake That Time Forgot. Shady trees hung eerily over the water. A scavenging raccoon surprised us when we stopped to put on sunscreen and eat lunch. Canoes back in the water, we explored Mud Lake. Its weeds and bulrushes sported all types of frogs, dragonflies, and mosquitoes. Out came the bug repellant! Mud Lake became our Florida Everglades. We wove our way through the weeds and a very narrow, shallow canal into River Lake, which we named the Sargasso Sea. Green algae floating on stagnant water covered our paddles as we adventured to the far end of this disconcerting waterway.

"Don't get stuck!" I yelled to the boys. "Or, you may have to get out and push."

Wrinkled noses, the boys acted like they were throwing up.

Our exploration time ran out too soon.

"We've got to go back now," I said.

"Dad, what about the fifth lake?" Jeremiah complained.

"You said we'd do them all," Mike joined in.

"The next canal looks like quicksand," I indicated with my paddle. "I have a better idea."

We retraced our way through the Sargasso Sea, the Everglades, and the Lake That Time Forgot. Then, at Sand Lake I yelled, "Man overboard!"

The boys and I jumped into the water, flailing, chasing, and dunking each other for half an hour while Joyce laughed. Tired, we climbed into the canoes and paddled back to the rental store.

Later, while roasting marshmallows and eating gooey s'mores around a blazing campfire, we shared stories of the day's adventures that erased any disappointment the boys had felt earlier. *Lord*, I thought, *I'm glad You're in charge. Thanks for an awesome family memory.*

Aaron M. Zook, Jr., a retired U.S. Army Colonel, delights in writing Christian music and books. His forthcoming Thunder and Lightning book series will take two adventurous boys and their talented canine sidekicks into worldwide mystery and intrigue. Aaron's music ushers the listener into God's work in his life.

Dawn Wilson

Peace in the Midst of Crisis

IN 1983, AS CORAZON Aquino rode a groundswell of national anger, Filipinos switched armbands back and forth, changing political loyalties. No one knew who they could trust. My husband was on a mission trip near the capital during the hostile political protests. When a military tank stopped in front of the compound with its gun pointed at the door, Bob rushed to stuff a small bag with emergency supplies for a quick exit over a bridge and into the mountains and jungle. But the jungle held its own danger with snakes and terrorist camps. Bob wondered which was worse, a tank or a terrorist.

Back home in California, waiting for a phone call, my apprehension surged as I watched news reports about the coup. When the call came, I told Bob about a television report that mentioned an American ship off the coast of the Philippines that was evacuating Americans.

Bob decided to call the American Embassy for help, but embassy officials told him, "You are on your own. It is the responsibility of your mission agency to get you out." That was a problem. Bob had no agency; he was the sole member of his own ministry. He looked out the window at the tank and prayed.

I prayed, too, more from fear than trust; and then the Lord spoke comforting words to my worried heart: "Your husband is entirely safe until I call him home." I exhaled stress as God's peace washed over me. Bob was secure in the hands of our Mighty God, whether in life or death. The sense of God's faithfulness was tangible. All that my husband and I needed for our time of crisis, we found in God's faithful presence; and as we filled our hearts with His Word, that sense of peace and presence overflowed.

During the crisis, I repeated one scripture for days: "You will keep him in perfect peace, whose mind is stayed on You, because he trusts in You" (Isaiah 26:3, NKJV). Whenever concerned friends and family called, I quoted that verse along with the words God spoke to my heart about Bob's safety. The God-focused overflow of my heart encouraged them, too.

The Lord kept Bob safe through the massive civil disobedience and the eventual leadership change in the Philippines, and we both rejoiced when he returned to San Diego. We shared lessons about how God revealed Himself in our time of crisis. We found that we can trust God's wisdom, because He gives guidance in tough decisions. We learned that we can trust God's love, knowing that He cares and has our best interests at heart. And we discovered that when all the props are knocked away, or when the enemy of our souls uses tough circumstances to try to steal our peace, we can always trust our faithful God and His good purposes (Lamentations 3:22-23; Romans 8:28).

Things and people can let us down, and circumstances can knock us down; but God never fails us. With His grace and strength, we can rise up to face anything, even a tank.

Dawn Wilson, founder of Heart Choices Ministries, co-authored the devotional book *LOL with God* with Pam Farrel. Her writing, research, and editing includes work for a number of national ministries and publications. Dawn encourages women to glorify and enjoy God and to make wise choices. HeartChoicesToday.blogspot.com; LOLwithGod.com.

Carolyn Marlowe

Shattered Pieces to Sheltered Peace

BROKEN DISHES LAY shattered on the counter and floor. I had collapsed while reaching to put a stack of heavy plates on a shelf. My mom rushed down the hallway to check the sound of breaking glass. The brokenness around me lay foremost on my mind.

While reflecting on the inestimable value of "broken things," I thought of broken things mentioned in the Bible. Broken pitchers produced ample light for the miraculous victory of Gideon's army; broken bread became more than enough for all the hungry; a broken box emitted fragrance to all the world; and His broken body became salvation to all who believe and receive the Savior (adapted from V Raymond Edman, *Who Said That*, George Sweeting, p 72).

Gideon, the least in his father's house, and men from the weakest clan in Manasseh, prepared to take command of outnumbered Midianite forces in Judges 6-7. Gideon and his men, trumpets in one hand and jars with lights in the other, surround the enemy's camp. As the men blow their trumpets and smash their jars, the *broken jars* produce ample light needed for the men to see and win the victory.

Matthew 14:19-21 unfolds Jesus feeding thousands with broken fish and a few loaves of broken bread. As He blesses and begins breaking the fish and loaves, the food multiplies. The crowds eat and become satisfied. The disciples fill baskets of broken pieces that continue feeding and satisfying the hungry. The *broken* bread and fish become more than enough for all the hungry.

A sweet fragrance emits from the broken box of ointment the woman pours on Jesus' head in Mark 14:3, 9. The Jews used ointment as a custom of the day to anoint honored guests. The woman considers Jesus the honored guest and anoints Him. Though costly, the fragrance of Christ radiates because of brokenness.

However many reasons for brokenness, it becomes beneficial when we allow the Lord to take our broken hearts and lives to use for His glory. I would know, coming from a home where broken relationships, broken hearts, sorrow, and pain seem to surface as the normal way of life. My dad's alcohol problem played a major role of our living in a state of defeat. My parents' divorce left my mom to become the stabilizing force for five children, taking us to church and introducing us to Jesus, while at the same time, working to provide for our family. School days become adventurous: cheerleading, activities, friends, and meeting my high school sweetheart, who eventually becomes my husband.

Years drift by; now married, I found myself in a depression. The days became long and lonesome, and the nights, a pursuit. Getting dressed became a great feat. The prescribed medication, though helping, had to cease because of my pregnancy with our second baby. Total dependence for my healing now rested in Christ alone. This route yields no disappointments.

The Lord taught me, through different sources, major avenues of why we spiral into this type of a depressed mindset. For me, I held anger and self-pity. He began revealing the anger held against my Father, for the childhood he put us through, anger against myself for some disappointing decisions I made, and anger against others for various reasons. He revealed the self-pity I carried, for growing up in a dysfunctional family.

Daily prayer became, "Lord, I cannot forgive, but You through me can." Learning forgiveness means *to untie*, I *untied* my Father, myself, and others from expectations built up in my thinking. The Lord also taught me, to offer up a *sacrifice of praise* for people and circumstances in my own life. Forgiveness began flowing. Self-pity began lifting. Life became renewed. My countenance noticeably changed. I emerged from shattered pieces to sheltered peace, as I realized, the Lord used every person and circumstance to cause me to recognize my need for Him.

Just as broken jars produce ample light to win the victory, as broken fish and loaves become more than enough to satisfy the hungry, and as the broken box emits the fragrance of Christ, Jesus gives victory and brings satisfaction to broken lives, with His fragrance through His broken body. Jesus heals the broken-hearted—out of the overflow of my once broken heart, now flows victory, deep love, great joy, and abiding peace.

Carolyn Marlowe recognized a famine of understanding the Scriptures in the church. She spent years studying the Bible, training in, and leading Bible studies. She writes Bible Studies, called Word Feasts, seeking to engage believers with the Scriptures. Carolyn is a wife, mother, writer, speaker, and interior designer. Visit www.WordFeasts.com

Valerie Goodwin

LIVING THE WORD

IT WAS NEVER meant it to be. I ran to the trap, falling to my knees beside him. His eyes fluttered up at me in shock. His heart beat fast, throbbing hard beneath his thin breast as much from fear as from his long exertion to free himself. But, he could no longer move. His feet and head were immobilized, his tiny wing wrenched into an agonizing angle from his small down body, caught fast in the dark tacky glue meant for a rat, but never meant to capture him.

This little one, created to fly upon the sun-split air high and free, now lay with a torn wing in something entirely alien to the life for which he was intended.

Praying for help so that I wouldn't hurt him more, I dug my fingers down into the gray goo under his wing, slowly separating him feather by feather from its grisly hold. Then I gently drew his head out and last his little feet. He was now inextricably glued to my fingers and my palm as I carried him into the house, wondering what on earth I could use to dissolve the glue from him and me.

I could feel his panic surge as he struggled in my hand at the sound of the water at the kitchen sink. I stroked the top of his head ever so softly with one finger trying to soothe him by my touch. I felt more tenderness than I could have ever imagined. With the water flowing soft and warm, I slowly edged his body into the stream. He panicked again, but as I began to gently massage the soap into his feathers he stilled, as it comforted him. The warm water flowing down his back and wounded wing seemed to calm him. He didn't struggle again, but let me do whatever I could, watching me the whole time through sad and sorrowful brown eyes. The soap was not strong enough to dissolve the heavy glue that adhered to his feathers, coating both his body and wing.

With growing certainty I began to mourn that he would probably never be able to fly again, or feed himself, or live the life he was meant for. I *had* to find something to remove this hideous stuff that would destroy him. Trying one agent after another to no avail, my sense of desperation rose.

"There must be something that will work! "I cried out loud, half prayer and half racking my brain for an answer. Slumping over the huge white sink, the baby bird still fast in my clasp, I agonized. "Oh, God, please, there has to be something that I can do." My heart was breaking, and I could feel the life beginning to ebb from his fragile spent body. His eyes closed for a few moments as if to rest, and then opened again to look into my own. "Oh, baby," I cried, wanting more than anything to find a way to set him free. His life was precious.

"Now, you know."

The deep resonance of *the voice* I know so well sounded in my soul, making me weak with just one drop out of the overflow of His own immeasurable pain and passion to find a cleansing agent to set his creation free. The blood. Oh, my Lord God, your blood.

Valerie Goodwin dreamed of the moment she would first lay eyes on her husband, two weeks before it happened. A Duke grad and women's Bible study leader, Valerie is always learning at her Father's knee.

Amy Wyatt

Joy in My Heart

I GLANCED AT the video camera and saw him jerking. Adrenaline rushed causing my heart to pound quickly. The clock flashed 1 a.m. and I tried to calculate in my just-awakened state how long it had been since I checked on my son. I started the timer on my phone and grabbed the rescue medication.

Running to his room, I wondered if we would be on our way to the hospital soon. I quickly turned him on his side and began talking to him. He wasn't responsive so I began to pray out loud. The seizure was not stopping and I knew it was time to give him his rescue medication.

Eventually the seizure subsided. He was spent and so was I. Angry, but relieved I sat down on his bed. This time, we had not had to call 9-1-1. This time we had not made the expensive trip to the hospital to stop a seizure.

But how many times had that very thing happened? So many vacations, birthdays, and holidays interrupted. How many sleepless nights? How much higher could the medical bills get?

I cried out, "Lord why is this happening? Why can't we get control? I don't know how much longer we can do this."

He whispered back, "My grace is sufficient for you. I am in control."

A song from childhood popped into my mind. "I do not feel like singing right now," I said to God. But the tune would not go away. It played over and over:

"I've got the joy, joy, joy, joy, down in my heart. Where? Down in my heart. Where? Down in my heart! I've got the joy, joy, joy, joy down in my heart, down in my heart to stay."

The song played on with I've got the love of Jesus and the peace that's promised down in my heart. It wasn't long before I was humming along to the tune. Slowly the fear subsided and the anger melted and peace and love took their place.

Riding in the car the next day, I questioned my son about what it was like to have a seizure. "Well, sometimes I know it's going to happen, but most of the time I don't," he said. "When I wake up and feel it starting, it's too late to call out because I can't say anything. Then I get worried and scared, and I wonder when you will come."

"I'm sorry you get scared," I said.

"It's OK, you always come."

"What's going on in your mind? What do you think about or feel?" I asked.

"It's sort of like a battle between my good emotions and my bad emotions," he said. "I'm really scared and I'm mad that I'm seizing, but then I hear you praying and I'm not scared anymore. Then it's like my good emotions win."

He was absolutely right. It was and is a battle. But God's love is what turns the outcome to our victory. Joy, love of Jesus, peace that's promised comes overflowing, winning the battle in the heart and mind of God's child.

Amy Wyatt is a wife, mom, writer and national speaker for epilepsy awareness. Find her at www.signsmiraclesandwonders.blogspot.com and www.EpilepsyAdvocate.com

Sandra D. Scott

PUZZLE PIECES

GOD IS A Master at constructing the puzzle of our lives. Only He can see the completed picture. As a child I assembled puzzles by starting with the border and matching the color patterns on the box. I got a rush of excitement finding the right piece and snapping it into place, joining little islands of partially completed pieces to the larger picture. No matter where the missing pieces are in our lives, God brings them together so we can realize who we are in Him and enjoy wholeness.

A few months ago God prompted me to revisit the *Prayer of Jabez*. The book reveals God's heart to bless those that ask Him. In obedience, though questioning why now, I started to entreat 1 Chronicles 4:9,10. Within weeks, my ministry in the prolife arena exploded. As an RN, I took a course for certification to do ultrasounds in a pregnancy center. Not much compares to watching the tense expression on a mother or father's face soften as they peek inside the womb to see their baby and hear its heartbeat. The impact of the prayer extended further, allowing me my first one-on-one counseling experience. I would be the last prolife contact for a young woman, scheduled to have an abortion the next day. She listened intently, without emotion, to my personal story of pain and grief that followed my two abortions. When she left, there was no indication my testimony helped her embrace her child. I learned, over a week later, her heart softened through God's grace; she chose life for her child. Puzzle pieces I thought useless, sorrow and shame; God snapped into place in a miraculous way.

A seemingly unrelated puzzle piece, my interest in photography, was rekindled during this hectic time of ministry. I researched Albert Stieglitz, a noted photographer, and his wife Georgia O'Keeffe, who brought to life the stark beauty of Abiquiu, New Mexico. A month later, I was startled to open an email from CLASSEMINARS about the 2010 writer's conference in Abiquiu. The guest speaker would be the author of the *Prayer of Jabez*, Bruce Wilkinson. My heart was tapped by a personal God.

From that moment I prayed for a financial provision. My idea was to improve my writing skills and take photographs of the stunning landscape. The Lord gave assurance of attending the conference through the Scripture, "Your eyes shall see the King in His beauty and your eyes will see a land that stretches afar" (Isaiah 33:17). The second part definitely fit New Mexico, but seeing the King in His beauty was a missing piece.

Shortly thereafter, my "territory" expanded as I joined the Silent No More (SNM) prolife campaign in Tucson. Scanning the SNM itinerary for the next month, I noticed Bruce Wilkinson would be the speaker for the Tucson Crisis Pregnancy Center fundraiser. God had my attention.

Mr. Wilkinson's simple message increased the faith of the audience to *just believe God* for the prolife work in Tucson. The end result—$920,000 was raised versus $180,000 the year before. Hundreds of believers left sure of God's ability to provide beyond their wildest dreams. At his book signing, I told him I would see him in New Mexico at the writer's conference. God provided a scholarship for me!

Puzzle pieces came together at the Ghost Ranch. My eyes were seeing "a land that stretches afar." I was about to see the King in His beauty.

As I left my first critique group, I noticed Bruce Wilkinson, sitting outside, sipping hot tea. I approached and reminded him of our encounter in Tucson. As we discussed the way God provided the previous month, the conversation naturally flowed to my story and recent healing. While I shared about receiving the Lord's forgiveness, Bruce asked if I had forgiven myself. That question triggered an exchange similar to Jesus' conversation with the Samaritan woman. Jesus made clear the simple truth of her needs. In that thirty-five minute puzzle piece encounter, Bruce guided me to truth, prayed with me, and understood my tears.

I saw my King beautifully snap into place my missing pieces to bring wholeness. Though bent, with frayed edges, I am complete in the Master and ready to be used to reveal the hidden picture in others lives.

Sandra D. Scott is a Bible teacher, registered nurse and newly published author. Her primary genre is children's fiction but has recently expanded to the pro-life arena. She has a passion for unveiling and ministering truth to women in the issue of abortion. She is willing to be transparent with her own story to help others needing healing and forgiveness, especially in the African-American community.

Alan Sherwood

Successfully Unemployed

I COULDN'T BREATHE! I struggled to inhale. A wave of nausea spread through my body. I had just received the news I was being fired as vice president of development and community relations for my state's largest hospital. Over the next several hours I felt anger, hurt, confusion, and disappointment at levels I never experienced before.

In that split second my life changed—more dramatically than I could conceive at that time. The loss was real. The devastation was immediate. My world instantly spun upside down. I felt sucker-punched; I literally lost my air. It was as if I had been hit by a truck, and I never saw it coming!

I had been promoted a year earlier, receiving more staff and responsibilities when two other vice presidents were laid off. Just one month prior, my boss, the CEO, had given me a superlative written and verbal evaluation. The day before I lost my job, the first little inkling came that something might be wrong. My boss, the CEO, walked through my office following our particularly tense evening board meeting. He simply said, "I'm not sure this is working. Perhaps we should meet tomorrow afternoon to discuss it." The next day my boss met with me. With little in the way of explanation or reason, he fired me. The "I'm not sure this is working," became "This isn't working."

Only two weeks earlier I got a book by Dr. James Dobson from Focus on the Family entitled, *When God Doesn't Make Sense*. And, yes, during the first week after my job loss, I read that book. It was needed and enormously beneficial. In time I became "successfully unemployed." Almost immediately, God brought an outplacement consultant into my life free of charge. He helped me to lose my anger, negotiate a better severance, and start to move forward with a comprehensive search.

Now I spend much of my time helping others experiencing job loss. Perhaps you are one of the millions in America looking for work. You too can be successfully unemployed! Ten principles reflect the attitude and direction of those who have truly been successfully unemployed. If you choose to embrace and implement these, you will experience a fulfilling search and will again be successfully employed.

1. Finding your dream job requires a life-changing job search.
2. View your unemployment as a transition.
3. Choose to remain teachable and learn from the valley.
4. Believe your sudden unemployment and job search have a divine purpose, even though you don't understand it, that the change can benefit your career, your character, and your life.
5. Start by preparing yourself - your heart, mind, and soul and by understanding yourself - your gifts, abilities, and passions.
6. Develop persistence against all odds. As Winston Churchill said, "Never, never, never give up."
7. Believe nothing has been taken away from who you are at your core; your values, your talents, your experience. Only your job has been taken away. One day soon you will be able to utilize all of this in another job situation.
8. Believe this could be a blessing, perhaps in not too deep of disguise. Look for the silver linings during this difficult period in your life. Learn more about yourself and what is really important in life.
9. Take advantage of this forced opportunity to think outside your occupational box and to creatively consider how to make a life rather than just make a living.
10. Be intentional about your life and your career. Finally, take comfort and strength from Jeremiah 29:11 which says, "For I know the plans I have for you declares the Lord. Plans to prosper you and not to harm you. Plans to give you hope in the future."

Though a difficult time in your life, it is nevertheless, a divinely-appointed opportunity. There are no accidents with God. This is for a purpose. Move forward by faith with the right mindset and skillset. In so doing, this may also become a life-changing experience.

During every step forward of my unemployment journey, my Lord brought me more help, hope, and healing. He offers you the same. You too can become successfully unemployed.

Alan Sherwood MBA, CFRE is President of Sherwood Consulting Service, Inc. He serves organizations with fundraising counsel and executive search services. Sherwood serves individuals by helping them find or create more fulfilling work through his speaking and career coaching services. For more information about speaking, consulting, or his upcoming book by the same title contact Alan at sherwoodconsult@aol.com.

Anita Agers-Brooks

More than DNA

LORD, HERE AM I! Send me. What message do you have for your servant today? I lay on the floor, face down before God, and prayed the combination of scriptures from Isaiah 6:8 and Joshua 5:14. On a warm fall Thursday morning, I couldn't know the powerful changes my fifteen-word request carried.

Hours later I received a Facebook message from an acquaintance, "Do you know anyone by this name?"

"I think it's my dad, why do you ask? I'm curious."

"Long story," she replied, "but I was adopted and my birth mother passed away last year. Right before she died, I asked her who my birth father was, and this is the name she gave me."

I felt my face flush. This wasn't what I had in mind when I lay prostrate before God and asked Him for a message.

I met my friend, and possible sister, two nights later for dinner and we compared notes. Afterward, we agreed we might be related. She wanted me to ask my father if he'd take a DNA test when I visited him the next week.

I hadn't seen Dad in a long time, my parents divorced almost thirty years ago, and much of that time we were estranged. However, three months earlier, God supernaturally planned a reunion for my father and me.

Nerves gurgled in my stomach at the thought of asking my dad to check paternity, but I agreed anyway. Later, I called my sisters from another state, to tell them the big news. One of them said, "Did you know they sell DNA tests at Walgreens now?"

"No," I said.

"I just read an article about it. You should check it out."

"Thanks, I will."

Sunday morning, before church, I once again gathered the courage to seek God's face in the prostrate prayer. I found a spot, and placed my entire body as close to the floor as possible. *Lord, here am I! Send me. What message do you have for your servant today?* I listened for a few minutes, and assured Him of my trust in His plans. I got up and went to worship as usual.

When I arrived back home, I called my Mom to discuss the recent turn of events. In response to my friend's request for DNA testing, Mom said, "I don't know if your dad will agree."

"I know, but if not, she and I can simply test as sisters," I said.

"I guess your brother could do it," Mom said.

We debated whether DNA determination required male/female samples. I sensed something strange, took a deep breath, and asked, "Dad is absolutely my father isn't he?"

Deep sobs riddled with forty-seven years of grief tore from Mom's throat. "I'm so sorry. I didn't want to hurt you. I've never breathed a word of this to a living soul."

When she finally calmed down, my mother shared a tragic story from her youth. She was hurt, and it left my paternity in question. She believed Dad was my father, wanted him to be, but needed to tell me there was a chance I belonged to someone else biologically.

The next day, I purchased two DNA tests from Walgreens, and carried them in my suitcase when I visited Dad. The first night there, I sat him down and dropped both bombshells in his lap. Because God healed our relationship in advance of my arrival, Dad agreed to the tests.

We mailed the samples off. On Friday, I took the leap and prayed on my face again. That afternoon I found out Dad is not my birth father. I didn't expect these results. However, when I told him, Daddy assured me, "You've always been my girl and always will be."

Oddly, I later found out my friend is not Dad's biological daughter either. We decided though, with our new bond, if we weren't sisters by birth we would celebrate our family heritage as sisters in Christ.

After all of this, I still fall on my face and ask the Lord, *What message do you have for me today?* His answers often surprise, but they comfort me. *I'm your Daddy. You are not an accident. I knitted you in your mother's womb. Fatherhood is more than DNA; it's the overflow of my Son's blood, alive inside of you. I'm sending you to spread the word.*

In the end, my experience taught me a new definition for DNA; God is Daddy-Now-Always.

Anita Agers-Brooks shares God's message as a Communications Specialist, Certified Personality Trainer, Certified Team Training Facilitator, public speaker, and writer. She lives in Missouri with her husband Ricky, and is the mother of two grown sons, with two beautiful grandchildren. Contact her via website www.freshstartfreshfaith.com or email anita.freshfaith@gmail.com

Sofia Simpson

Washing My Feet with a Toothbrush

I FELL ONTO the couch of my new rental home. My whole body felt like a wet noodle. With a little over a week's notice, we were forced to move. It was the day after the move and I had just gotten off work. When the phone rang, I thanked God it was near me.

Seeing my dear friend's name on the caller ID, I answered gratefully, "Hello?"

As I looked around all I could see were boxes. It had been two days since my husband and two young boys moved in, and I was overwhelmed.

"Do you need any help unpacking?" my friend asked sweetly.

"Jenny," I replied, "You just worked all day, and you don't need to help me unpack."

Despite my staunch refusal, she replied, "I'm coming. Will you be home in an hour?"

Knowing her penchant for gentle stubbornness, I relented and said, "Yes, but under one condition. You will not unpack, just see my new home and have coffee with me."

"Ok!" came her shrill voice, and I knew there would be a fight of wills. Exhaustion overtook me. I did not have the energy for this. I had moved out of my home and into a new one in one day, in addition to working a full-time job and managing this new change with my two boys, seven and four.

She arrived right on schedule, but I was late even making the coffee. She took one look at me and said, "What can I unpack?" Mustering up a reserve of energy I didn't know I possessed, I said, "Nothing. You do not need to do this. Let's just have a cup of coffee and see what happens."

Looking at me with steely eyes, she answered, "No. I want to do this. I'm going to unpack something." And then she asked me again, "What do you need unpacked?"

I felt like a boulder had plunged me down to the bottom of a sea. I was weightless, yet burdened with complete weariness. The sea was now a raging river of pride, and right then I knew the Lord was asking me to allow Jenny to serve me.

I looked over at my new home's very dirty pantry and said, "I need my pantry boxes unpacked, but the pantry is too dirty to even use."

After walking in and evaluating the area, she came back with her hands on her hips and said, "Do you have a toothbrush?"

I looked at her, dumbfounded. "A toothbrush?"

Gazing at me patiently, she said, "Yes."

"No!" I yelled, "This is too much. Here is a dishrag and disinfectant spray. I don't know where anything else is. But, please don't ask for a toothbrush to clean my entire walk-in pantry!" And," I continued, "You have a bad back. Please do not work too hard, Jenny!"

Smiling sweetly, she took the dishrag and spray and walked back into the room. I watched, horrified, as she ignored my plea, got down on her hands and knees in her business clothes, and began to clean.

"Go and get your cup of coffee and sit and talk to me."

I reluctantly followed her orders and dragged a chair over to her work area.

As I watched my friend scrub, one thought dominated my mind. It was a Bible reference, and as surely as if my shoes were off with a bowl of warm soapy water at my feet, Jenny reminded me of the woman who washed Jesus' feet.

My dear friend was "washing my feet" in complete servitude. And I realized another thing. The Lord had put that desire on her heart, not mine. My idea of serving me was to just have coffee.

She asked for a toothbrush.

Sofia Simpson is proud to serve the Lord as a wife, mother, writer, and children's librarian for the Mulberry, Florida Public Library. She has been married for ten wonderful years and has two very smart boys, seven and four, and a cat who thinks it owns the house.

Sheryl Samson

A Second Chance on Super Bowl Sunday

WHAT POSSESSED ME to think I could minister through music in a prison? Inside a maximum-security federal prison, the rigid bars on the security gates slam in slow, synchronized movement. Walking with my ministry team, we were getting deeper into the prison's environment. One door closed, leaving us caged in. Realizing that we were cut off from the natural world, I was apprehensive of the unknown, feeling nervous, and fighting an urge to turn around and run. I was sharply aware of the strong smell of institutional bleach. The vast concrete floors blended into the walls, making a tunnel effect.

We entered this harsh place prayed up, realizing this was a calling, not a convenience. I remembered Hebrews 6:19, "We have this hope as an anchor for the soul, firm and secure." I knew I could share God's hope, as it overflowed within me. We kept walking down the endless hallways toward the prison's auditorium, not knowing what to expect.

First we met with the Chaplain and a few Christian inmates, who expressed their heartfelt petitions for others to know the saving grace of Jesus Christ. As we settled into the auditorium, inmates were led in and the guards stood at four corners of the room. Although the auditorium seated 200, only a third of the seats were filled, but we had prayed that God had brought the men that needed to hear His words of goodness.

As we sang our first song, this "captive audience" was already standing and clapping. The reaction was great. At the fourth song, I felt a strong tug from the Holy Spirit saying, "close the concert." With forty minutes left in the concert, it could be confusing to alter the agenda, but I knew it was the Lord's direction. The trio looked confused, as I began sharing a message from my heart.

I said to the inmates, "This might be the last time you have the chance to accept Jesus as your personal Savior. The Lord is mindful of each one of you—where you are and who you are. Jesus came to save everyone from sin. Your life counts, no matter what you've done. Jesus died for you, and if you believe it, receive it with me." I prayed a simple prayer, asking them to repeat it with me.

Once that was completed, there was no reason not to continue on. As we began the next song, the house lights went on unexpectedly. A group of guards marched in to exit the inmates. Instead of leaving, the inmates began to crawl over the theater-type seats, like waves of prison issued khaki-tan clothing being tossed in the air and flowing toward us. They didn't want to leave. Now, they wanted to hear more of God's Glory.

We were herded into a locked cage for protection. The curious wonder on our faces had the guard telling us, "read about it in tomorrow's paper." As we were escorted out, I knew the seriousness of the moment—officers were in riot gear, holding rifles. We were out of the prison in record time.

Later I read there was a stabbing death on the inmates' yard. The dead man had been invited to our concert that Super Bowl Sunday, but he said "no" at the last security call. Instead, he chose the path that led him to death. None of us know how our days are marked off on God's calendar.

One of the Christian inmates sent us a note, relaying the excitement that occurred after we left. During lock down, the cells were active with men recalling the message of God telling them "it may be the last time to accept Jesus." That afternoon, with the man's death lingering on the forefront of their minds, many began accepting Christ into their lives, knowing it could've been them on the yard that day. Heaven was pulled down to remove the hell within their lives. Something happened much more important than a Super Bowl game. What was meant for destruction was now a platform for second chances. My heart was overflowing with the truth that God is the God of second chances—even on a Super Bowl Sunday.

Sheryl and her husband, Chaplain Randy, work actively in prison ministry. Since 1981, Samson Ministries has had the privilege of ministering throughout California, with Sheryl performing as a singer-songwriter. The ability of sharing all that the Lord has given in story form remains a constant joy.

Andy Savage

PRAYER AT THE RED LIGHT

I HATE RED lights. This morning I was leaving the gym and got caught at a red light. Normally this kind of inconvenience would simply be one more thing that adds to the morning stress and another reminder of my impatience. However, this morning was different. It dawned on me to take the opportunity to pray. I wish I could take credit for this pious idea but I was far too concerned about my agenda for the day. This was the Holy Spirit reminding me of what's really important.

So, I decided to pray, the only question was, "what in the world should I pray about?" Immediately I was impressed to simply pray for whatever I see on the four corners of the intersection. On the first corner I noticed a local bank. I prayed people would be treated fairly. Perhaps a Christian employee would be a bold and respectful witness for Christ as they interact with fellow employees and customers. Next I prayed for an insurance office. I immediately thought of the many in crisis who would call today needing help to process a car wreck, a house fire or the loss of a loved one. I prayed that their calls would be met with grace and kindness. Next I prayed for a church. This particular church was a bit run down and I wasn't sure if anything was still going on there. I prayed that God would revive the excitement and passion of the pastor and congregation to reach hurting people and make disciples here in our city and beyond. I couldn't make out what was tucked behind a group of trees and landscaping on the fourth corner but prayed whatever the business was that God's kingdom would come on earth as it is in Heaven.

This simple exercise raised my expectations regarding prayer in the most mundane of moments. Imagine if our faith in God would overflow from our lives even when faced with an inconvenience. Imagine what God may do if we all prayed at red lights. I believe

God may expand your heart to see fellow drivers as people God loves and for whom Jesus died. I think our concern for our city would grow and help us see beyond our personal agendas. Maybe we would long to see God bring help and salvation to those we pass by every day. Perhaps we may even experience what Jesus experienced in Matthew 9:36-38.

"When he saw the crowds, he had compassion on them, because they were harassed and helpless, like sheep without a shepherd. Then he said to his disciples, 'The harvest is plentiful but the workers are few. Ask the Lord of the harvest, therefore, to send out workers into his harvest field.'"

The light turned green I said, "AMEN" and for the first time in a long time I drove away thankful for a red light.

Andy Savage is the teaching pastor of Highpoint Church, a dynamic congregation in his hometown of Memphis, TN. Andy is married to Amanda his wife of nine years and has three boys. Andy's passion is to speak, teach and write to make God make sense. www.andysavage.net

Leah Clancy

Rules Worth Singing About

MY SMOKIN' HOT aerobics instructor once told me she would trade her body and the grueling work she had invested in it for a nice singing voice. I have to say I would do the same, except I am missing a hard body to use as collateral.

Technically, my voice is okay. My problem lies in the area of pitch. Thanks to my husband's gift of honesty, I am aware I have a tone deficiency. My mind knows songs require specific notes, but my vocal chords prefer to choose their own.

My grandmother tried to help by funding voice lessons during my high school years. To her dismay, my one and only concert was terrifying for both me and the audience. Consequently, I decided to implement a set of rules regarding acceptable singing practices.

1. Never, under any circumstances, sing without back up music unless you are alone.
2. "Happy Birthday" is completely off limits. Mouth the words instead.
3. If you must sing in the presence of other people, do so quietly.
4. On the rare and wonderful occasion a band is blaring, you are standing next to family, and no one is in directly in front of you, you may sing loudly (ex.: an actual concert or the youth group worship service).
5. Under all costs, avoid risky conversations about favorite songs that could require a rendition of the song in order to jog the other person's memory. (They wouldn't be able to identify it anyway.)

6. Only lullabies and Sunday school or silly kid's songs sung to children under the age of 10 are acceptable.

I've adhered to these rules religiously, and they served me well until one Sunday morning when God decided I needed to fine-tune my thoughts on the whole singing matter. Worship service had just started. Following along with the praise team, I opened my mouth to sing, when I heard a woman's voice screeching the words "holy, holy, holy." I almost choked on my gum. It was obvious this wounded crow was unaware of "the rules."

After I regained my composure, I truly felt sorry for her. She was embarrassing herself and making me uncomfortable. How could I concentrate on God's love with all that squawking?

Once again, I opened my mouth to sing, when the words to "Merciful and Mighty" came bellowing over my shoulder, making me long for a purse-sized BB gun to put this bird out of her misery.

Finally, as we got to "All the Saints Adore Thee," God had had enough. He began to have a talk with my heart. He let me know I was being harsh and self-centered. If there were actually singing rules, I was the one breaking them. The precious soul behind me sounded like a lark to Him and He was beaming at her decision to praise Him full force, despite what people might think. I began to soften, as I pictured God smiling at the tiny, singing crow in his hand.

Suddenly, the bold voice coming from behind sounded like a lark to me, too.

I now have a new hobby. I thoroughly enjoy shocking unsuspecting church goers with my squawks of praise, despite the red faces of my family.

> "Worship the Lord with gladness; come before him with joyful songs."
>
> —Psalm 100:2

Leah Clancy is a pastor's wife and wrangler of four spirited children. She ministers alongside her husband by teaching, speaking, and hosting various events. With her southern humor and transparent style, Leah encourages women to bravely conquer fears that starve a fruitful life. She can be found at 21piecesofbrave.blogspot.com.

Sally Walls

His Graduation

UNABLE TO SLEEP, my husband Jim heard the quiet, gentle knock at the front door. With grave faces, two police officers delivered the message that would turn our happy home into a rubble pile. "Is your son named Davis Walls? He has been killed in a traffic accident."

A week earlier, we had celebrated his high school graduation. It was a joyous marker moment in our lives, full of praise for Davis's past efforts, and filled with hope and dreams for his future.

In a heartbeat, the words of Psalm 38:8 became my story, "I am feeble and utterly crushed; I groan in anguish of heart." Nothing could have prepared me for the loss I felt. When you lose a child, you also lose potential grandchildren. You can lose your will to live as well. Shattered, my emotional lifeblood leaked out of me. I awakened every morning to the sound of my own mournful cries. Each night I prayed sleep would free me from the agony of having to live another day without my son.

Slowly, the Holy Spirit began to renew my spirit and restore my life. But every day, I intentionally chose to live for God, trusting He would provide just enough to see me through so I could show up for my husband and young son, Owen.

Just days before Davis died, he had one last project to complete at school. The fine arts assignment required he find a poem, an excerpt from literature or song lyrics that defined him. Little did we know how significant this would become for us. He came bursting in after searching for days on the computer, waving a piece of paper in victory, stating he had found the perfect poem. He took each one of us aside and read it aloud. "The Battle," written by J.L. Zumbrum, powerfully describes the struggle between God and Satan and the decision we make for all eternity when we choose our side. Davis's eyes shone as he read, "I hear my Savior knocking, He's standing at the door and all the earthly worldly things aren't important anymore!"

Rewinding the tape, we realized Davis gave us his last testament that evening, only days before his glorious graduation to his heavenly home. He died on the weekend before he was to share the poem in class but hundreds of students heard it read at his funeral, just as he would have wanted.

Years earlier, while Davis was in fifth grade, God whispered to me that I would write a book about my son. I treasured God's calling in my heart but was puzzled. Davis's death brought this fuzzy picture into a clear focus. God had prepared my heart to trust in His faithfulness, even through tragedy. Though the circumstance of Davis's death could not be changed, our hearts could. Jesus continues to transform our brokenness into wholeness. A healthy home now flourishes where a rubble pile once stood, "beauty has been formed from the ashes" (Isaiah 61:3).

Sally Walls has not been a spectator to loss; she has been fully engaged. Throughout a decade of heartache, God has shown her that He makes good on all of His promises. With a passion for encouragement and a relational heart, she has been involved in women's ministry for over 20 years, has been a frequent guest speaker and attends Centre Street Church in Calgary. Sally, her husband James, and teen-age son Owen live in Calgary, Canada. Their other son, Davis, now lives in heaven.

Ruth Ann Dalley

AN EMPTY VESSEL

I STILL DON'T know put the large postcard in my mailbox. It didn't have an address; it was blank. It advertised the 2009 Christian Writers Conference from CLASSEMINARS. *Who are they? Should I go?* I hadn't celebrated my birthday since my husband passed so I gave myself a birthday present. In August I took a step of faith and signed up for the conference. God touched my soul and heart at the conference. *Listen to me, listen to me.*

I felt the strong presence of the Holy Spirit as I soaked up everything I heard, at every workshop I attended. Attending this conference was a pivotal point in my life. Searching for God's will at the Christian Writers' Conference led to God awakening my soul by overwhelming me with His love and acceptance. I left the conference with the gift of joy and the knowledge that I wanted to write devotions, children's books, and young adult novels.

I departed the conference inspired to write, but when I returned home so did my daily challenges, ready to greet me at the door. The little slice of heaven I experienced shattered. Even as I traveled from heaven to reality, God's reassurance comforted me for I knew He would give me the desires of my heart and use them for His purposes. Still, His timing proved different than my own. Though disappointed, my faith grew stronger again and I knew I had to obey Him.

President of CLASSEMINARS, Gerry Wakeland's, mantra was "Pray and wait; wait and pray." This charged me to slow down and expect a clear answer to my prayers at His timing rather than mine.

Stressed, working hard, struggling with obesity, battling many other health problems, exercise, and trying to slow down my fast paced life so I could hear God. Seven years ago, I became an empty vessel when my husband and mother died within three months of each other. Without him I felt adrift and floating through life, unprotected from the storms of problems that followed his passing. My cry to God was, *why didn't you take me too?*

I didn't know what to do as I stumbled my way through the grieving process, so I hid behind my workaholism to block out my sorrows. I was too busy or too exhausted to listen to God. Still, I heard at times when God whispered to me, "Be still and know that I am God."

I was made in God's image and I'm sure he isn't obese. Facing the truth, I found a program through a friend that stressed a healthy lifestyle rather than a diet. I lost 29 pounds and, with new habits, have kept it off. I gave up my favorite foods (bread, potatoes, rice, and pasta) and after three months, my craving for these foods diminished tremendously and my hunger pains vanished.

With God's help I also faced that dreaded word again…exercise. My physical trainer, Kelly, had a business card with a Bible verse from 1 Corinthians 6:19-20 on it. "Do you not know that your body is a temple of the Holy Spirit, who is in you, whom you have received from God? You are not your own; you are bought at a price. Therefore honor God with your body." This verse led me to create my praise walk that I do each day. Near the end of my walk, I surrender to Him and ask Him to fill me with the Holy Spirit so I can be a blessing to others.

Addressing my problems has given me the freedom to focus on my writing. To prepare for the 2010 writers conference I wrote up a storm instead of creating one. God's inspiration helped me to daily surrender to Him. My days flow and a deep satisfaction fills my heart. King David says in Psalm 27:13-14 "I am still confident of this; I will see the goodness of the Lord in the land of the living. Wait on the Lord; be strong and take heart and wait for the Lord." My empty vessel now overflows with God's will for me.

As a native of San Diego County, California for 37 years, Ruth Ann Dalley now lives in Poway, the city in the country. As a retired teacher, Ruth Ann likes to knit items for babies at the local Children's Hospital. Her companions are two Tibetan Spaniels, Tawnee and Joy Joy, who are small watch dogs.

Cynthia A. Rogalski

MARVELOUS GRACE

GRACE—SUCH A short and sweet word for such a life-changing gift. God's grace is always surrounding me. Even before I realize my need, He has already supplied the person, finances, or even the tiniest detail.

God's latest blessing has become apparent this year. I started to entertain the possibility of pursuing writing in 2004, but put that idea on hold. He reignited that desire by making it possible for me to attend a one-day writer's seminar in June of 2010. God provided me with the finances, the vacation time, a supportive husband, and most importantly, the self-confidence to do the road trip, which I hadn't done since college many years ago. That seminar sparked my desire to do what God had for me to do; to use the gifts and talents He has given me to reach others for His Kingdom. Knowing our financial status, I could not see any way I would be able to attend a week-long conference 2,000 miles away. God started to move and impressed upon me that I needed to go. One by one, God has eliminated each obstacle and excuse I could manufacture not to attend.

Then, twenty-two days before I was scheduled to leave, my husband slipped while hunting and ruptured the quadriceps tendon in his left knee, requiring surgery and many weeks of physical therapy and recovery. The enemy of my soul could not attack me spiritually, but will use whatever he can to get me to take my eyes off of what God has set before me. In this case it was physical and emotional. How could I leave my beloved to go traipsing off to a writer's conference when he needs me to care for his needs and drive him to the doctor and therapy? Only God's grace could have enabled him to progress as far as he has. Only God's grace has relieved the pain enough for him to take less pain medication so I don't have to worry about him losing his balance while getting around with a walker. Only God's grace could have allowed me to recognize Satan's false guilt regarding this matter. This same grace is allowing a glimpse of what God has for me; enabling me to conquer my fear of travelling alone, flying for the first time, boldness to dream of a different career path and daring to stretch into the new experiences awaiting, using the talents and gifts He has provided for only me.

Trusting in His grace has allowed me to take my eyes off of what I can do, and focus more fully on what He can do. And not only what He can do, but what He *will* do. Each step of this journey with Him is so amazing. He sends people I couldn't have imagined to encourage me. And He doesn't stop with one or two—I have been the recipient of so much, I can actually feel my heart filling, indeed, overflowing. His mercies are new every morning. He has promised there will be more. Marvelous grace.

Cynthia A. Rogalski is a sculptress, storyteller, and author. She resides in Easton, PA with her husband Jack and is the mother of two adult children, Justin Mabee and Lindsey Barrett. Their other three children, Bristol, Mollie and Jesse each have four legs.

Ramona Springer

The Unexpected Storm

THE STORM WAS brewing, it was October and we had just completed a year in our new home in a very rural area. It was taking some getting used to - the dirt roads, no lights, and the posted speed limit of 15 miles per hour. My husband, Louis, youngest son, Mark, and I had agreed to meet at 9 p.m. at the house. It was a 20-mile drive to town. I telephoned and, to my surprise, no one was home to take my call.

About 30 minutes later I received a call from Mark, who said his father was being air-lifted to the hospital. On his way home, my son happened upon an accident about three houses from our home—police, ambulance, and helicopter present. He was asked to find another way home, but a gut feeling told him to question the authorities. He felt that it was his father, and he was correct. Once he identified his father, he contacted me and went to look for his brothers to go to the hospital.

Upon our arrival, the doctor came out to let us know what was wrong with Louis. His vehicle's sunroof had scalped him from the top of his head to his middle back. Surgery was going to take at least six hours, if not longer. They needed to make sure all the dirt, glass, and rocks were cleaned out, and we were told he had a 40-percent chance of survival.

He came through the surgery and was placed in ICU.

I once heard the Lord calms the storm for His children, and that sometimes He calms the children in order to get through the storm. The Lord did the second for me.

I walked around that hospital for 11 days like a zombie, even though I felt like I was doing well. On the twelfth day, my eyes were opened and prayers were answered. As I prayed and surrendered my husband to the Lord, a peace overcame me. I went into the ICU again and asked the Lord to embed into Louis's heart the two things he needed most:

how to show love and how to accept love. The man was 45 years old and didn't know how to do or accept either.

They moved Louis to a regular room and then to rehab a day later. Louis had to relearn everything: how to chew, swallow, talk, use the restroom, and walk. He wanted to go home so badly, but rehab was the only way he would be able to return home. To everybody's surprise, he was walking in a little over a month.

I dropped him off at rehab one day and received a call within an hour to inform me that he "wasn't cooperating well with the therapist or the doctors." I returned and settled him so he could finish rehab. That went on for a few weeks until, by no other choice, we had to take him out of the program. Because of this setback, I took over rehab until he was capable to perform tasks on his own.

It has been 15 years since that horrible accident, and my husband has since accepted the Lord and learned how to love. He still needs a little help now and then, but he has shown love to his grandchildren and has accepted their love unconditionally. Louis is now learning to do the same with our sons. I have asked the Lord about this very thing, and His answer has always been the same: "In My timing."

It hasn't been easy, but no one said it would be. Our Lord is bigger than all of this, and it will all end well—and in His time.

Ramona Springer worked in the CLASSEMINARS office from 2005-2008. Now she serves as a volunteer with CLASSEMINARS ministry. You can most frequently find her behind the book table selling books. She is a Certified Personality Trainer and Bible study leader. She and her husband Louis have three sons, three grandchildren, and live in Albuquerque, NM.

Carolyn Hunt Watson

DIFFICULT TIMES

THE LAST FEW years have been difficult for me. My mother has advanced into Alzheimer's disease, leaving my brother and me to share in the responsibility of her care. We have watched a beautiful, independent lady deteriorate into a fearful, fragile stranger.

Many nights I cried myself to sleep while listening to her unintelligible conversations. I wrestled with impatience when she poured her glass of iced tea into the green bean casserole. I fought embarrassment when she insisted that the restaurant's napkin and fork were hers. I struggled with anger when she stubbornly resisted to change her soiled underwear. Everything about her care was exhausting and emotional.

When professional care became necessary, my brother and I cried together as we filled out required papers. Then we faced the difficult decision to sell her house—the only childhood home we had ever known. We grieved together over resurrected memories of our happy childhood.

During our ordeal, we remembered Job's struggle through devastating losses. Messengers waited in line to deliver bad news. Job lost his family and possessions, yet he continued to trust God. His faithful example is encouraging to my brother and me. We know that the God who loved Job is the same God who loves my brother and me. We will continue to trust God with our own difficult days no matter how many messengers are in line with bad news for us. God is still good.

Carolyn Hunt Watson has taught in public schools for 20 years. She is the wife of, Gideon, a United Methodist minister, has two adult sons, and a one-month old granddaughter. Carolyn has written a children's book, *The Smell of Love,* and her second book is ready for publication.

Cindy Teel

The Overflow of a Grateful Heart

IT WAS A particularly difficult day at school. My students were boisterous, and I was extremely tired. I just wanted to get home and relax in a quiet spot. When the cell phone rang that afternoon, I had no idea that my day's difficulties were about to increase. It was my grown daughter on the other end telling me she was in the hospital, which is several states away where she lived. Lately, she had hinted about some minor health issues she was experiencing, but I had not been alarmed by her descriptions. I learned she'd been in the hospital since midnight the night before. As she described the battery of tests the doctors wanted to perform, I knew immediately they were looking for something serious, specifically cancer.

I tried to remain upbeat and positive on the phone and told her to call me back when she had more information. When I hung up, I quickly called my husband and relayed this information to him. To my surprise he had spoken to her much earlier that day and was already driving to join her. He volunteered to turn around and come back to get me, but I knew that would be a waste of time. It was a ten-hour drive and it would just delay him more. So, as he traveled on to her, I was left alone and rattled.

I immediately cried out to God not really even knowing what to say. My mind began to race and I could not focus. He drew me to Philippians 4:6-7 NKJV, "Be anxious for nothing but in everything by prayer and supplication, with thanksgiving, let your requests be made known to God and the peace of God which surpasses all understanding will guard your hearts and minds through Christ Jesus." I needed that peace desperately, so I immersed myself in those words.

The word "nothing" is actually a compound word made up of the two words—no and thing. He was telling me to be anxious for NO thing—not even a health crisis for my daughter. "But Lord," I argued, "How can I not be anxious about this—it's too big?" The Lord promptly impressed upon me it did not say "Be anxious for NO small thing;" it said "NO thing." As I pondered this verse more, I realized the way to this peace I longed for would begin *with thanksgiving*. I knew my cries to God must originate in a grateful heart. I began to think of everything I could thank Him for in this situation. My daughter was in a large city with a wonderful university medical center, okay, I could thank Him for that. She was not in a lot of pain and she also had good health insurance. She had not been taking care of her health and this could be a wake up call for her—and the list began to grow longer. My mind was racing now with things I could be thankful for. As I changed the focus of my prayers from "woe is me" to "thank you, Lord," I noticed a change in my heart. No longer was I anxious and having that nervous feeling in my gut, but I began to feel God's peace flow into my heart. How could I be so calm in the midst of this storm, especially since my natural bent was to worry? The more my heart was grateful, the more the peace flowed. It was beyond my human understanding.

As I marveled at what God was doing, I remembered I once learned that the word *guard* in this verse was a military term. It referred to a wall that surrounded many ancient cities and protected the inhabitants from the enemy. I realized the peace I was experiencing was *guarding* my thoughts from racing and my emotions from roller coasting much like a soldier guarding a city.

Eventually, my daughter was given a clean bill of health, but immediately I was given a gift. It began with gratitude and ended with the overflowing of God's peace. Anxious times will come into our lives, but I've learned to choose gratitude to replace anxiety. So pour your heart out with gratitude and He will fill it up and overflow it with peace, *the peace that surpasses all understanding.*

Cindy Teel is the co-host of "Girlfriends," a women's talk show, airing on Legacy TV. She also serves as a speaker with the On Fire Ministries Team. Her passion is to teach women how to apply the Bible to their everyday lives. As a recent graduate of New Orleans Baptist Seminary, Cindy is eager to serve wherever God leads.

Annie Pajcic

Emergency Landing

THE TWIN ENGINE Cessna's hydraulic line exploded. Bright blue fluid covered the pilot's hands as he tried to manually pump the landing gear into place. My heart kicked into full speed as I saw him place the tattered Emergency Instructions in the window of the cockpit. *What's happening? Are we going to crash? Am I going to die today?* Oddly, everyone remained silent until the Captain turned around with calm reassurance and said, "Don't worry. I've done this before."

Done what before? My mind was spinning as fast as his lips were moving. He was communicating with ground control, and I quickly began communicating with heavenly control.

My husband and I were on our way home from celebrating our eighth wedding anniversary. Our romantic, peaceful get-away was jolted into reality when we began to smell gas in the small plane. Being the only passengers, I quickly questioned him, "Curry, what's that smell?" He sweetly dismissed my fear, and pointed down to an incinerator plant that we were flying over in St. Thomas.

But I knew better. I knew something was wrong.

In traumatic times like these, they say that your life flashes before you in an instant. Whoever "they" are, they are right!

As the pilot was quickly proceeding with emergency protocol, I felt suspended somewhere between surreal, rewind, and fast forward. *Could this really be happening?*

If my life was on trial, would I be convicted of being a follower of Jesus? If we were to meet face-to-face today, would He say, "Well done, Annie. You have accomplished my will for you and you have glorified me with all that I gave you?"

The barrage of questions, choices made and life yet to live, became overwhelming as we circled the airport one more time.

The report was clear, our landing gear was in fact, NOT intact. An emergency landing was in order. I saw the chaos of firetrucks and ambulances lining the runway as we made our final loop above the serene, calm Caribbean ocean. The pilot dumped all the fuel in the ocean, turned off the engines, and everything became strangely quiet.

That's when it happened.

That's when I felt the supernatural overflow of the Holy Spirit take full control of my body. My shaking stopped. My heartbeat slowed and I heard the still, small voice of a purposeful, powerful God.

"You are not going to die today, Annie. I have much more in store for you."

Curry looked at me. It was time. One last glance into his precious eyes, and I knew my knight in shining armor loved me more than I could ever understand. He laid his body over mine--and we landed.

Smoke filled the tiny aircraft and the sound of steel meeting tarmac was deafening. The sudden stop took longer than expected when I heard, "ABORT SHIP!"

"They" say you do silly things in traumatic situations. I did. I looked cute when I boarded the plane, and I was going to look cute when I left the plane. I grabbed my lunch, my purse, and did what I was told. I aborted ship. I didn't see Jesus face to face that day, but I did come pretty close to a six-foot, aluminum dressed fireman. He zipped me around a firetruck, into a white SUV, and it was over. And I fell apart.

When life gets stressful and the pressures of being a mom of four become overwhelming, I ask God to take me back to that day. I imagine myself in the plane where I have to completely surrender my agenda and undeniably trust that He is in control.

Are you in a place where you need to surrender control? Do you need to be reminded that God is the pilot of your life, leading you in the direction that He wants you to go?

God promised the Israelites in Jeremiah 29:11, "'For I know the plans I have for you,' declares the Lord, 'plans to prosper you and not to harm you, plans to give you a hope and a future.'"

That same God reminds me that no matter what happens in life, He has a plan and it is good. It might not look good, feel good, or smell good. But it is.

He is the directional Pilot of my life, turning around to whisper with calm reassurance, "Don't worry, Annie. I have done this before."

Annie Pajcic has 15 years of professional graphic design and illustration experience. Her background in classical ballet and full-time ministry brings a unique blending of art and God's Word. She has created four Bible studies for tween girls and an artistic ministry called Thouartexalted.com. She is married with four children.

Charles Short

God's Spring Glory

Birdwatchers love the spring. Sparrows, warblers, and wrens stop skulking around in the deep cover of brush and grasses and begin to display themselves in plain sight. They call out as if to say, "Look at me! Listen to me!"

Their audacity is really God's glory. It is He who placed within them a calling to find a mate, lay eggs, and perpetuate the species. This crooning and cooing for a mate is also dangerous; high above are the hawks and falcons waiting for the small and vulnerable to expose themselves. The dangers are real; so are the rewards.

Some birds will succeed in finding a mate and joyfully return to their secretive ways. Others will die trying. Some of their fears will overwhelm God's call. They will preserve their lives, but will never know the joy of finding their God-given purposes.

Perhaps what I define as calling is merely instinct. Instinct is nothing more than God's instructions to the animal. I believe God's instruction is God's call.

Seems so easy for them! We wrestle with discerning where God is leading and what He wants from us, for us and to do through us, while for them God's perfect intent flows from life's natural patterns. Too often, this is where we mess up. We expect God's leading to be profound and important. God *will* call us to the deeply meaningful and eternally significant, but *first* He calls us to the commonplace and the simple. Our obedience in lighter matters opens the doors for Him to call us to weightier matters. Matthew 25:21 (NASB) says "*Well done, good and faithful slave. You were faithful with a few things, I will put you in charge of many things; enter into the joy of your master.*"

We presume when God's call arrives it will be something big. In the meantime, we live for ourselves. After all, the little details of our lives don't seem significant since God has not yet revealed a higher purpose. What strikes us as minor issues of doctrinal clarity, moral purity, and consistent integrity are all postponed while we wait that momentous opportunity.

And yet, every moment is important. Our character is God's first priority. This is a part of our call. We assume we can scrape together the necessary character at the point of need, like a student cramming for a test. So we wait for and desire some higher call, and wonder why it has tarried so long in coming. But while we wait among the dried twigs of a compromised life, we miss the higher call to be sanctified.

Here are three steps to create greater personal potential in God's kingdom. First, strive for moral obedience in every instruction from God. Take all His teachings as a serious part of your calling. Study Scripture so as to understand the intricacies of your doctrine. Find a congregation and commit yourself fully to its work. Consistently sacrifice your selfish will for the higher calling of personal purity.

Second, be very careful to live courageously for Jesus. The dangers are real. We will certainly attract the enemy's attention. But we are called to risk our lives for Jesus sake. It may not work out like you hope, but that is not the same as failure. It is the next step in God preparing you.

Third, don't believe you are unworthy, unusable, or unsuitable for God's purposes. We are all aware of our own shortfalls. But in our weakness He is strong, for His perfect plan is worked through our brokenness. God's calling is never a mistake, but it does require your cooperation, or dependence, on Him.

When you fight your way through these steps a transition will take place. Your heart will come to be full of the things of God. You will love what He loves; you will hate what He hates. Don't be surprised if the new character formed in you also creates an ability to see how God will use you to change the world.

Allow God to complete His perfect call in you. Not by biding your time waiting for that big opportunity, but by living for Him in every moment. Then one day, when your heart is filled to overflowing with Jesus, your joy—and His—will be perfect and complete.

Spread your wings and soar, you were made for this.

Pastor Charles Short has been at his current church for ten years, and in the ministry for twenty. He always considered that some day he would publish devotionals, but recently God has called him to write a book to help Christians unlock their potential through a better understanding of heart.

Cynthia Carpenter Thomas

General Revelation

As I reflect on my
bucolic surroundings;
In the chatter of life,
these are my groundings.

Thank you, Lord,
for fresh country air;
Wildlife resting
in secluded lair.

A harvest moon
with starlit skies;
And a knowing
that the sun will rise.

Springtime flowers
and the bronze of fall;
Summer heat
and the coyote call.

New calves born
and a mother's milk;
Corn stalks tall
with kernel and silk.

Dry creek beds
and streams that flow;
Frost on the meadow
and flakes of snow.

Beaver biting
bark off of logs;
While deer stand
in the hazy fog.

Woodpecker works
with a rat-a-tat-tat;
And a field mouse flees
from the old barn cat.

Porcupine quills
and rattlesnake warnings;
Roosters crow
in the dewy mornings.

The hoot of the owl
and the axis call;
The hills echo
the sounds of it all.

Breezes bending
tall, dry grasses;
Elm sap drips as
thick as molasses.

The scent of smoke
from burning embers;
And sunrise glowing
through standing timbers.

Cycles of life,
seasons of earth;
In the still of the night
there is a new birth.

A songbird swoops down
and spreads the good news;
God reveals himself
and man must choose.

Cynthia lives on a ranch and finds solace in God's creation. She expresses her observations and emotions through the poetry that flows from her pen. Trained by Peacemaker Ministries, she enjoys sharing the biblical principles of peacemaking. As a graduate of Dallas Seminary, she is eager to teach God's Word. cynthomas@yahoo.com

Sheri Mackey

Out of the Overflow and Into the Deep

OCCASIONALLY IN LIFE, we are called to dive deep into dark and stormy seas. As our son continued to sink further into bipolar depression at age 16, despite our continued attempts to rescue him, we were in just such a place. We were exhausted and felt defeated, however as we looked up from the gloomy depths, we saw the bright light of God shining down. The surface of the turbulent sea seemed so far above our heads, but we knew as He reached His hand down into the depth of our despair that Jesus would bring healing and goodness to our broken hearts. He knows of hopes and dreams that have been lost at sea and He weeps with us as we seek safe harbor from the tumultuous waters that are our lives. As we overflow with sorrow and feel defeated, Jesus will always come to our rescue - if only we ask.

Often, as we descend into the depths, it is difficult to remember that we are God's people, His children, and He knows we are furiously bailing water as our small, insignificant vessels rapidly submerge. When we come to Him with an open mind and a humble heart, He will not only repair our small boat, He will fill the holes in our heart and in our spirit to overflowing. Our sorrow will become joy as He challenges us to go into the deep - to use what He has graciously given us to help others on His behalf. As we set sail in turbulent waters with the knowledge that we are privileged to have a loving Captain navigating on our behalf, God's nautical compass guides His great plan for our lives. We go to the deep as we realize that our life - our plan - is shallow water when we begin to comprehend the depths of the purpose God has for each and every one of us. Going into the deep does not require us to know the specific coordinates on the map, but it does require us to have unwavering faith in the internal compass God has provided that is unique to each of us. It requires that we commit to having the confidence not only to keep our eyes on Him within the shallows of our own lives, but also as he takes us into the deep—walking on water to find and save those lost at sea. He desires us to go far out into the turbulent waters of life, beyond ourselves, to find room in our hearts for those in need. In this we actively extend the life preserver that is our trust in Him. We maintain faith to reach out to others in times of trouble so that they, too, can know that Jesus is a safe harbor in every storm for everyone who asks. God desires for us to go into the deep and seek those adrift at sea—He asks us to find them and bring them to Him.

As we venture into the deep, we are blessed both by the overflow of joy and sorrow in our lives—one is not effective without the other. Jesus graciously uses both to equip us to go into the deep in His name.

Just as we are taught in Psalm 42:7, "Deep calls unto deep."

Only out of our very personal overflow can we be called—we are God's unique life preservers, sent to save others in moments of greatest need on His behalf - there is no greater honor. Out of the overflow Jesus ensures our hearts are steeped in hope, mercy, and the desire to go forward in His name so that we can find the compassion to go into stormy seas and extend a helping hand—His hand - in troubled times. Because God's love overflows in our lives, we go fearlessly forward.

As my Captain, Jesus provides me with the perseverance to navigate safely into the deep. My faith resides in Him …and out of *that* overflow I have the capacity to go forth and seek those adrift at sea, serving them in Jesus' name.

Even as we continue to be tossed about in rough waters, the Lord has provided a respite for us to breathe and we are secure in the knowledge that we have safe harbor in the arms of the Lord as we continue to go into the deep…for Him.

A leader with over 20 years global experience, Sheri Mackey is the CEO of Luminosity Global, an executive coach, a speaker, and a writer. She is an Internationally Certified Master Coach, has an MBA in International Management, a B.Sc. in Psychology, leads missions with her husband, Steve, and mentors at-risk teenage girls.

Ashley White

The Dance

I DANCED WITH my lover this morning!

Standing on the side of the old gym with my tattered heart and worn out dress, I sensed a gentle breeze moving towards me. I glanced up to notice Strength, Beauty, and Royalty closing the distance between us, and His gaze was fixed on me. With each step He took I heard the crackle of the wooden floor beneath His feet, and there was purpose and passion in every step. The softness in His eyes beckoned my soul, and the melody of the music stirred my heart. As He approached me the breath of His Presence was sweet and intoxicating, and I was in awe that He had chosen me—the least of these!

He extended His strong yet comforting hand, and without a word I placed mine in His. As we embraced I felt His warmth, and I was keenly aware that I was His. I followed His lead and was completely unrestrained. With every step I became more like Him as He twirled me around the dance floor to the music of the waltz. Oh how He delighted in me. As His hand was nestled in the small of my back, His strength and grace upheld me. He was the most amazing dancer, and I was the beauty of the ball in His arms. It was the first time in my life I was not on the side; I was on the floor and my heart was alive.

The music began to fade, and my heart longed for more. I did not want this dance to end. Not then—not ever! Then suddenly He drew me close, twirled me out, twirled me in, dipped me back, and brought me close to His heart again. He knew my every thought, my every fear, my greatest desires, and my every wound. Just one encounter with Him had brought healing to my brokenness, set my feet to dancing, and enticed my heart to more. I was free!

This is what it means to be alive and beautiful! This is true romance. Priceless jewels had been buried deep within me, and at last my lover was removing the veil. After encountering My King and My Prince, one dance simply wouldn't do. I had believed the lies far too long, and it was time to come out of hiding. It was time to step into everything I had desired and everything for which I had been called. It was time to be free, and dancing in His arms I would be. For there, I no longer had "to do" a thing, I only had "to be." "For I am my Beloved's and He is mine."

Breathless and tearful I opened my eyes and rose up from my living room floor. Desperate for an encounter with My Savior, it was there, that I had hit my knees only moments ago. "What in the world was that?" I thought. What had I just experienced? Immediately I thought back to my high school years, and the Friday night dances. I remembered the anticipation and the longing for just one invitation to dance, or just one to delight in me. I can see myself standing there in my beautiful dress yet no one ever came - never! For an innocent searching heart this was a deep wound I buried and tried to forget. In reality, it would color and shape every decision I would make. So there in the middle of my deepest longing and greatest brokenness He came for me. And I heard Him say, "It is time for you to live! Living is in the dance. I have come for you, My darling, now dance with Me!"

This was my first dance, but it will not be my last. Dancing into freedom is daily, personal, and one step at a time. Encountering Him in such a way has changed my life, and it will change yours.

Are you available? Will you take His hand? For His invitation is personal and continual. Trust that His heart towards you is good for He delights in you. Let the music play, and follow His lead one step at a time—straight into freedom.

He is calling…Listen…

"Come My darling, dance with Me - again and again and again!"

Ashley White is a speaker, prayer coordinator, and resource writer for On Fire Ministries. On Fire Ministries is a ministry for women and teen girls. On Fire Ministries is the parent ministry to "Girlfriends" Christian women's talk show. She is a wife and mother of two children.

Sheri Mudge

Peace In the Storm

HAVE YOU EVER gone through a stormy season in life? My life has been marked by the devastation of divorce. Through this storm, turmoil can manifest itself in unique ways. Encounters of fear, anxiety, and shame lurk around every corner. These emotions like to strike at the most unforeseen times and destroy all peace.

On a recent cold and dreary afternoon, dark clouds of grey filled the sky. It happened while quietly sitting at my computer. Boom... an emotional storm abruptly hit. I read an unexpected email and the next thing I knew, all serenity blew out the door.

I cried out loud, "I so don't want to do this today. I don't want to deal with this and I don't want to feel this." But my mind was already entangled. We all get stuck at some points in our lives. Here I sat, stuck again.

So, I laced up my tennis shoes and headed out the door. Walking is my outlet. Maybe if I walked far enough, my racing thoughts would disappear.

One foot in front of the other, I started off along my favorite trail. It hugged the sandy beach on one side and the tall rugged cliffs on the other. With the cold breeze in my face, I started to release my worries to God. I prayed..."Help me Lord!"

A battle raged in my soul as I humbly plead my simple prayer. I would pray, then zap.... take back control by rehearsing the email over and over in my mind. Fear and anxiety overwhelmed me. Held captive, I was a prisoner to my own thoughts.

Through my mental chaos, I persevered in my three-word prayer. I didn't stop. Amazingly, it was as though I closed my eyes and when I opened them God emerged.

His presence, in the sky, surrounded me. Patches of white and grey clouds triumphed across the blue heavens and led to bright hues of red, yellow, and orange. The colors engulfed the horizon. I stopped in my tracks, grabbed my phone, and snapped some pictures.

As I reflected on His stunning creation, my mind filled with wonder and awe. The image before me was bright, big, and powerful all at once. God had my full attention.

Through the brilliant rays of light He proclaimed, " I am God Almighty. Do not worry. I know your pain. I see you. Look to me. I am all around you. I am here."

Despair diminished. The very act of focusing on God's power and glory took my eyes off of myself. My mind transformed into one of gratitude and praise.

As I approached the end of the trail, I glanced up in the opposite direction. To my delight, perfectly set in the sky hung a colorful rainbow. Once again I stopped in awe. A big grin came across my face. God gently whispered, "And by the way… you can trust me, I promise you."

Oh precious Lord! Thank you for your promise that in the midst of the storms of life, my heart can be filled and overflow… with your peace and presence! (Psalm 19:1, Philippians 4:6-7)

Sheri Mudge is a mother of three and lives in San Clemente, Ca. An aspiring writer and artist, she is currently working on her certificate in Expressive Arts Therapy and pursuing her Masters degree in Marriage and Family Therapy. She enjoys reading, oil painting, and walking on the beach. sherimudge@gmail.com

Delores Liesner

SWEET SURRENDER

THE DOOR SWUNG open and I stepped back in shock.

I barely recognized my former coworker, Patti. Her face and bald head were scarred and swollen from medication. The only hair the brain surgery and chemo had left was a limp rooster-comb patch that drooped above her forehead.

I silently mourned every missing strand of her signature chin length blond tresses. Looking into her familiar blue eyes, I found the friend and co-worker who had called the day before saying, "I think you have what I need."

Now those eyes gleamed in eagerness and her familiar voice echoed from within the distorted body that, even she quietly admitted, was no longer recognizable as her own.

"Save visiting for later," she said; those few words emphasizing, as clearly as if she'd written them across her classroom chalkboard, that she knew she was dying and had no time to waste.

Three portions of scripture had come to mind as I prayed throughout the 45-minute drive to her home, but now I stood mute and stunned before her grace.

The sight of her struggling to hand me a huge maroon large-print Bible snapped me to attention. I pulled a TV table next to the sofa and set the Bible on it. Patti smiled, touched the book reverently, and said, "Show me."

I pointed out John 5:24 and she slowly read the verse, her fingers lightly tracing each word with love. When she came to "no condemnation" she let out a gasp of delight and clasped her left hand to her heart.

In my trance of empathy, I was about to go on to the next verse when her other hand wrapped itself around my wrist in a desperate grasp and she cried, "Wait—get a highlighter!" Surprised, I rose to the table she indicated and returned with the fat yellow marker. The tumor, she explained, was affecting short-term memory, and though she might forget who visited, or if she ate lunch, she did not want to forget God's words. Once the bright yellow outlined the words for later reference, she sighed, momentarily contented.

"OK," she said, like an eager child, "I'm ready now for the next one." Her voice rose in excitement reading 1 John 5:11-13—especially the portion that stated, "These things were written that you can know that you have eternal life." When she read the word "know," she held the edge of her cushion excitedly, as if she would leap off and dance.

"I can know, I can know," she chanted.

"I don't have to wonder or to hope anymore—I can know." Reverently, I watched as she marked the verse. Then she surprised me by reading it again, this time putting her name in place of the word you, now reading in wonder, "I, Patti, can know."

Her happy laughter was contagious, and I sat back and joined her, watching her face glow with joy.

Finally we looked into the first chapter of Ephesians and talked about all we have and are in Christ. Our tears mingled as we hugged and prayed, and then talked about the goals she wanted to reach before she died and ways they could be accomplished.

We visited then, singing and praying with abandon until her family arrived from work. Humbled and awed as I drove home, I replayed Patti's sweet surrender to the Lord and her excitement and reactions to verses and concepts I had known for years and perhaps had begun to take for granted.

Though she asked me to come to give her comfort, I realized then that in the face of her overflowing joy I had also been given a gift, for I knew I had lost the fear of death. It was gone, and with certainty I could even tell why - there simply was no room for it - it had been replaced, pushed out, overcome by the reality of the power of God's Word. Caught in the tsunami of Patti's joy and assurance, God's presence had washed over her and spilled onto me.

For once I did not care that I couldn't carry a tune, and wove my way home singing "The Wonder of It All" through my tears.

Delores Liesner has hundreds of stories published, including a column (Prime), *Chicken Soup for the Soul*, "Ultimate Series," "Kiwi," "Focus on the Family," "Woman's World," "CBN.com," and *Guidepost books*. Despite an abusive background, Delores believes God offers hope and humor in every life circumstance. Contact at deloresliesner.blogspot.com or lovedliftedandled@wi.rr.com.

Craig and Robin von Buseck

God Laughs

I DIDN'T KNOW that God laughs. He is God! He's busy running the universe. After all, He is watching all that we do, especially the stuff we don't want him to see! This was my view of God.

As a single parent, life was hard. I believe I always wanted and needed God in my life. I prayed and talked to God sometimes, especially when I needed things. But I was a little afraid of getting too close because I understood that He knew every bad thing about me.

On one particular fall day I was happily cleaning house. The children were in school and I was off work for that day. This was a rare treat, as my life was busy with a full-time job and kids. I heard a knock on the door. There stood two women from a nearby church who were giving away bread and doughnuts. Yea! Yum. They asked if I had children, "Yes, I do," I replied. They gave extra. Then they left without even telling me what church they were from.

As I unloaded the goodies they supplied I thought about these kind ladies. Suddenly the desire that had been burning inside of me to attend church rose to the surface and lingered. Later that day, while visiting my mother and sister, I shared the event. My mother told me of a new church that had just begun in my old elementary school. I asked her, "Will you go with me? I want to go to church, but I don't want to go by myself."

My little sister spoke up and said, "I will." So that following Sunday my sister and I visited this new church together.

I was nervous and excited. That day changed my life. That's how it all began. I couldn't get enough of Jesus.

Many amazing things happened during that time, but one in particular really stands out.

One night I was sound asleep in my bed—and I am a very sound sleeper. Somehow I was sweetly awakened. I got out of bed and was drawn to the nearby window. I stood there gazing at the countless stars shimmering in the nighttime sky, the beauty of Him, shining through the darkness. Wow. Suddenly a star shot across that sky in a lingering blaze and I heard my Father's voice say, "I." It was as if he put his finger on the star and spoke as he pulled it across the heavens. My eyes followed that star as it traveled all the way across the horizon and faded into the darkness.

I looked back up as a second star slowly crossed the same path while God spoke the word "love." I was awed, and I said to Him, "God, you don't have to make the third star fall. I know you are going to say "You."

He answered, "I know I don't." Then he gently laughed. I looked up as the third star shot across the sky with the sound of my Father's voice speaking the word, "you."

I thought with amazement, "God just laughed? God laughs! And he loves me more than the stars."

I wandered back to my warm, snuggly bed and drifted right back to sleep. The next morning I couldn't believe I went back sleep after such a visit. I wrote the words "Three shooting stars and I love you" with the date in my Bible.

Even today I am amazed as I look at the great shining stars in God's heaven and remember His love and His laugh. We are as the stars and the sand… we, His children. He loves us, and hey, he laughs.

Dr. Craig von Buseck and his wife and partner in ministry, Robin, live in Virginia Beach, VA. An ordained minister, he holds a D.Min. and an M.A. in Religious Journalism from Regent University, is the co-host of CBN.com's Spiritual Gifts webcast, and author of *Netcasters: Harnessing the Internet to Make Fishers of Men.*

Rosalie Schwarm

YOU ARE SO GOOD TO ME

YOU ARE SO Good to Me is a title for a song that flowed from my heart at the most unlikely of times.

En route to my best friend's mother's funeral in Sarnia, Ontario, I had sufficient time for contemplation driving the two-and-a-half hour stretch along the Trans Canada highway.

The quiet hum of my silver van seemed in sync with my thoughts as I reflected on the passing of a godly woman whom I admired. Her servanthood, her sweet, gentle smile, and her obvious abandoned love for her family, would be deeply missed.

She had loved and emulated Christ. Now, in the "twinkling of an eye," Marie had been changed and was clothed in glory.

You are so good, Lord, I mused.

As I contemplated the thought of my friend Marie's body being lowered into the grave, thoughts of my life began to arise. Flashbacks of sin, crime, and lawlessness flooded my mind as I envisioned all Jesus had done for me. I was so grateful to remember how God had redeemed me out of the grave.

Suddenly an overwhelming sense of gratitude took away my breath as my spirit and soul overflowed in weeping for the joy of the Lord's generosity and grace toward me. I started to breathe the words, "Oh Lord, you are so good to me! You are so good!" One by one, the words took on sounds and unexpectedly, a song began to flow from my heart.

I praise Your Name, and lift You high
I praise the One that rescued me and gave me life.
I lift my hands, I lift my voice
I praise the name of Jesus Christ, who is my Lord
I'll be ever grateful to You Lord for the sweetness of Your love
Your tender kindness and Your mercy, that You never once withheld
And I just want to say...

Chorus:

You are so good to me My Lord,
You are so good to me, my Lord,
You are so good to me....
My Lord.

A teenage rebel, runaway, and kleptomaniac, Rosalie Schwarm embraced the life of a Goth until her collision with God. Through divine intervention, she immigrated to Canada from Australia to become established in a new life in Christ. Rosalie is now a pastor and conference speaker based in Burlington, Ontario. www.gotlight.org

Cynthia Leepper

THE IMPOSSIBLE IS POSSIBLE WITH GOD

"For with God nothing is ever impossible and no word from God shall be without power or impossible of fulfillment."

—Luke 1:37

TIM BURTON'S 3D movie *Alice In Wonderland* is the story of a young woman who feels constrained by her aristocratic lifestyle. She escapes to a fascinating world of strange creatures where she experiences dangerous adventures. The danger begins when Alice and her new friends are chased through the forest by a giant beast known as the bandersnatch, which has razor-sharp teeth and claws. Alice believes she is dreaming, so she stops running and faces the bandersnatch saying, "You can't hurt me." The beast stops, and stands still as if it had become powerless because of Alice's words.

My cell phone rang as I was driving in the city with the news that one of my client's real estate transactions had fallen apart and wasn't going to close. My disappointment quickly turned into prayer. I pulled into the nearest parking lot and declared to the universe, "The Word of God says that I will eat the fruit of my labor. This deal will stay together, and I will get paid for my work." Miraculously, everything worked out and I was paid for my work at the closing.

Just like the fictional Alice, Jesus used words to create miracles. He spoke and a Roman Centurion's soldier was healed by His words from many miles away. Fig trees, storms, and fevers were obedient to His commands. Everywhere Jesus went people marveled at the authority of His words. And just before He ascended to Heaven, He delegated this authority to those who would carry on His work in the world.

In Mark 11:22-24, Jesus told us to have faith in God, to speak to obstacles in our lives without any doubt. He said that while we are praying we are to confidently believe it is our Heavenly Father's will to grant us whatever we ask of Him. The Bible tells us of the woman with the issue of blood, who intercepted a healing miracle by believing and saying she would be healed by simply touching Jesus' clothes, and it happened. She asked and He gave.

The devil and his demonic army oppress God's children very much like Alice in Wonderland's Red Queen and her wicked cohorts oppressed the White Queen and residents of Wonderland. At the end of the movie, as Alice battled the enormous fire-breathing, dragon-like Jabberwocky monster, she confidently spoke these faith-filled words:

Sometimes I've believed as many as six impossible things before breakfast. Count them, Alice...

1. Drinking something can make me smaller.
2. Eating something can make me larger.
3. Animals can talk.
4. Cats can disappear.
5. There is a place called Wonderland.
6. I can slay the jabberwocky.

Alice proceeded to slay the jabberwocky, which brought freedom to all the inhabitants of Wonderland. Alice spoke positive faith-filled words that made the impossible, possible.

Here are just six of the impossible promises of God for His children found in the Bible...

1. God is always with us.
2. All things are possible for those who believe.
3. No weapon formed against us will prosper.
4. Jesus came that we might have and enjoy life abundantly.
5. Whatever we do prospers.
6. We are overcomers, more than conquerors, and always triumphant.

When my real estate deal needs help or my physical body needs healing, I can either pray and talk about my problem, or I can pray and talk about my desired solution for the problem. The Holy Spirit continues to amaze me every single time He causes me to overcome any difficulty I may undergo.

Jesus called us God's precious beloved children, and He made it clear our Daddy-God can make the impossible happen for us if we will simply believe and ask Him. He sent the Holy Spirit to partner with us so we can use our faith-filled words to bring glory to the Father. In the Wonderland movie, faith-filled words were the reason Alice experienced victory in every dangerous situation. In reality, our confident faith-filled words can bring about victory for us in every situation to bring glory to the Father. Jesus declared it: nothing is ever impossible for him who believes.

Cynthia Leepper provides practical ideas for the victorious Christian life. Her passion is ministry for those with a desire to experience God's presence and blessings in their everyday lives. Cynthia speaks and writes about faith that embraces the sufficiency of God's instruction and His truth. She demonstrates how prayer changes things for those who believe all things are possible with God.

Virginia Johnson

Out of the Overflow of God's Mercy

ONE MORNING I awoke in my second-floor bedroom and readied myself for the day. I ambled slowly down the stairs to the main floor of our home. I am a night person and ambling is the best I can do in the morning. As I rounded the corner and entered the living room, I found a baby bird sitting in the middle of the floor. Inside my house! How strange! How in the world could a bird have entered into my living room? There were no open doors or windows to provide entry, and the chimney flue had been permanently sealed. It just didn't make sense.

I gently caught and examined the little creature, then released him out the front door. With unexpected urgency, I felt compelled to identify the bird. I was able to determine that it was a mourning dove. Hmmm. How interesting!

I gave it little thought as I continued my busy schedule. Three days later, when following my morning routine, I rounded the corner into the living room. This time, I discovered my husband's lifeless body. Surely this was not happening! It was not possible!

Sometime in the days that followed, in the midst of the confusion and numbness, God drew my thoughts to the little bird. In scripture, God's Holy Spirit is described as descending like a dove when Jesus was baptized, so a dove is often used to represent the Holy Spirit in Christian circles. It was then I realized that God was speaking to me in my thoughts, "I was in this room three days ago, when I revealed my spirit to you with a dove. I was in this room in the early morning hours when your husband chose to take his life. And I will always be in this room and beside you, as you work your way through the healing that I will provide."

The days that followed were spent struggling through the aftermath of the death of my husband at his own hands. Disbelief, numbness, shock, and anger abounded. Unanswered questions flooded my mind as unbridled emotions surged from within. Where was God when this happened? Surely He knew what was happening. Why didn't He intervene? How can I face the world? How could I continue living? Scarcely able to function, I began the agonizing grief-journey toward recovery and healing.

Out of the overflow of His abundant love and mercy, God provided an innocent dove, a *mourning* dove, as reassurance that in the middle of crisis and catastrophe, He is there. Just as He was there in the beginning, He will never leave or abandon us in our time of need. Thus, new meaning was given to me regarding the promise and encouragement in Hebrews 13:5-6. "I will never leave thee, nor forsake thee. So that we may boldly say, 'The Lord is my helper, and I will not fear what man shall do unto me.'" (KJV) Because of God's wondrous overflow of love and compassion, I must take the abundance of mercy He gives me and let it flow to others who need Him.

"For just as the sufferings of Christ flow over into our lives, so also through Christ our comfort overflows" (2 Corinthians 1:5 NIV).

Virginia Johnson, Ph.D., is a professor at Biola University, La Mirada, California, and teaches Educational Psychology and Child Development in the School of Education. Following the death of her husband in 1998, Virginia assists others as they restore stability in their lives in the aftermath of suicide.

Melissa Mashburn

More than Enough

EXHAUSTED, WORN OUT, and just completely bone dry. Day after day beaten down by the not enough's, not trendy enough, not fast enough, not skinny enough, just plain not enough. The hardest part of it all was that the not enough's were coming from my church.

Imagine dedicating your life and ministry to Kingdom work only to be under the constant pressure of meeting the impossibly high deadlines and expectations of others. On top of the intense demands placed on those in ministry, my own need to have things just right and desire to please others poured into a toxic work environment.

Leave it all on the field, don't let one thing get by you, be everything to everybody and do it all with a smile. This mantra is simply impossible. The day finally came, when regardless of my good intentions, all the spinning plates came crashing down. My life and my ministry took a drastic turn.

Stepping away from everything that was a part of this chaos was not an easy choice, nor did it prove to be simple, but when push came to shove it was absolutely the right thing to do. When you have nothing left to give others and you have completely wrung yourself out what comes next for some is a season of sitting on the bench.

In Matthew 11:28 NLT Jesus says, "Come to me, all of you who are weary and carry a heavy burden, and I will give you rest."

Rest. It sure sounds easy, but when you are used to running at a hundred miles an hour working sixty hours a week trying to chase after these gigantic goals it really is hard to simply slow down. It takes time to allow your body to come out of that cycle, but that is exactly what your Heavenly Father wants. He wants you to sit down and really seek Him.

One afternoon I grabbed my Bible, my journal, my coffee and went outside to sit. I honestly had no idea of what God was doing, but I knew I needed to sit there. I sat there for four hours. Crying out and begging God to reveal Himself to me in a new way was something I had been missing from my life for many years.

It was during that day I began reading His Word with a hunger I could barely remember. I felt closer to Him than I have in years. He was there waiting for me to just sit with Him. That's what He had been wanting all along—just for His daughter to come and sit with Him at His feet.

Meeting with Him day after day allowed for a time of healing, growth, and renewal - I could feel that my cup was finally starting to fill back up. The season on the bench lasted for longer than I would have guessed but I could see that He was taking the time, day by day, to prepare me for this next season of ministry.

Each day I grew stronger my cup started to get close to overflowing and I simply said to Him, "put me in coach, I'm ready to play." I knew that my season on the bench was ending and that He was calling me back into ministry at another church. But this time, I knew something that I didn't know before: I can't share the grace, mercy, and love of Him with others if I'm not taking the time to make sure my cup is full.

With a hunger and desire to keep Him first in every single part of my ministry: I served, loved, and cared for His people again with a genuine passion to see them feel His love as intensely and freely as I do...just as I am, which is more than enough for Him.

Melissa Mashburn is a pastor's wife, mom, writer, and speaker. She's also founder of Mel's World w/Melissa Mashburn (www.MelissaMashburn.com) and the series Godly Gals, where she encourages women to take their everyday, ordinary lives and place them as their offering to God.

Diane McGovern

Deep Heavenly Focus

I'M HAVING TROUBLE breathing!" said my 22-year-old daughter, Elizabeth, who was home for spring break from college. She'd developed a severe viral lung infection and her lungs began to collapse in places. Her doctor gave her a fifty-fifty chance of survival. For days, she teetered between life and death, and we didn't know if she would live.

From the moment we heard her discouraging odds, the Lord raised up a massive prayer team on her behalf. He showed our family how to go to His place of refuge through Scripture and prayer. He'd carried us through three tumultuous days. On the night of her third critical day, I planned to stay in her room until 2:30 p.m. I asked the Lord what I should do when I was there, and He clearly prompted this thought: Sing worship and praise songs. The song "Blessed Be the Name of the Lord" came to mind. I loved this song the first time I heard it. It reminded me of the promise God made to Israel through Isaiah "Behold, I will do something new, now it will spring forth; will you not be aware of it? I will even make a roadway in the wilderness, rivers in the desert" (Isaiah 43:19, NASB).

I'd sung the song with gusto many times before Elizabeth got sick, but I had to ask myself, *Did you really mean what you sang so many times before, or were you just mouthing words? Is your faith and love for God deep enough to actually sing and bless the Lord at a time like this? Your daughter could still die.* While I examined my heart, I remembered the time a mature believer told me that when it's dark and bad, that's the best time to praise God, even if it seems radical or ridiculous. The urge to follow God's leading grew stronger, so I yielded to the Holy Spirit's control.

I quieted my heart and began to sing any chorus or hymn God brought to mind. I really began to enjoy the singing. The longer I sang, the stronger my focus grew on the Lord. As I sang, I felt a new kind of strength. Later, when I took a break, I was surprised to feel so overwhelmed by joy. It followed me out of her room and down the ICU hall, giving me extra energy. Since my repertoire of songs was running low, I asked God for more ideas. The chorus, which starts out, "The joy of the Lord is my strength," floated across my mind, so I began to quietly sing those words. This joy became incredible. It mounted within me more and more by the minute. As I walked back to her room, I snapped my fingers and hummed another line or two.

Once back in her room, the Lord quickly drew me back into intense worship. I closed my eyes. The heavenly focus God gave me was complete, and it felt like no one else was in the world except God, Elizabeth, and me. Between songs, a holy stillness filled her room. Time stood still. When I tried to comprehend what was going on in her room, the Lord brought another verse from the Bible to my mind "Yet You are holy, O You who are enthroned upon the praises of Israel" (Psalm 22:3, NASB). I realized God was enthroned upon my praises. God stirred my heart to sing using bold words that spoke forth His greatness. As I sang, I placed God in the highest place of authority over our lives. The sovereign Lord sat on His throne in that ICU room. He'd been right there with us all along, and I believed somehow Elizabeth was worshipping along with me in her spirit. That night, I experienced the deepest, most focused worship of my life. It was awesome. As I drove home, I couldn't contain the joy of the Lord. It overflowed.

Elizabeth survived and lives a healthy, full life serving God. Through my daughter's health crisis, I discovered our new life from God comes equipped with abundant joy, even in the worst of times.

Diane McGovern was a stay-at-home mom while she and her husband of thirty-one years raised three daughters. She also led women's small group Bible studies for eleven years before joining the leadership of Bible Study Fellowship for four years where she occasionally rotated as a teaching leader.

Andrea Chevalier

Desert Overflow

I WOULD HAVE never described the desert as a place of overflow—far from it. The first experience I had with a desert can be summed up in two words—hot and dry. It was not a place I was by choice. It was part of the destination. My family had been on vacation in California, and the only way to get back to Texas was through the desert in Arizona.

My next experience with a desert came four years later. This time the desert was even more dry and painful because it was not a desert I could easily drive through and go on to my destination. This desert was a personal one. It was a dry time in my life when everything familiar in my life had been stripped from me. My husband had recently lost his full-time job, and we were left to live on my part-time teaching salary. This drastic income loss forced us to live an hour away from the school and our friends, and I looked around at the mess I now called my life and wondered, "Where is God in the middle of this?"

Over the next several months of that spiritual drought, God began to show me that my thoughts were all wrong. Although I pictured overflow as splashing and swimming in an ocean of abundant blessings, His picture for me of overflow was bringing me to a dry, desert place where I would be forced to empty myself. Only after this pouring out of myself could He fill me to the point of overflowing in Him. It was really what I had asked for all along; however, I did not recognize God's unique packaging.

This became crystal clear to me one afternoon when my overflow was tested at the ultimate place for a parent—a conversation with my daughter. She sat at the kitchen table with tears streaming down her face and asked, "If God is really as faithful as you say He is, then why has He not given Daddy a job?"

Without really thinking, I began to list for her all the ways that God was being faithful to us. We had food to eat, clothes to wear, and shelter. We were in need of nothing—maybe "in want" of a few things, but certainly not in need. Then I got out my Bible and started showing her story after story where God had proven Himself faithful. We prayed together and she walked off feeling better because of our conversation.

As I sat in my chair praising God for our time together, I realized that God had just overflowed to Audrey through the things that dry, empty me had learned. I was able to show her all the things I had been using to remind myself that God was faithful and was going to carry us through this time in my life. If I had not been in the place I was, I might not have been ready to help strengthen her where she was. Only He can take the bad and overflow it into something good.

Andrea Chevalier is a teacher and motivational speaker with CLASSEMINARS. She resides in Houston, Texas, with her husband Gary, and two daughters, Audrey and Allison.

Chad Spriggs

SET FREE

A son brings home his bride to be; they're in love they're so free
Set free to love and live unfettered, hopes and dreams that make life better,
To grow and birth a life together the joy, the fear that makes life's letter.

Years of joy mixed with pain test the dreams young love contained.
Poisoned blood now fills his veins its venom casts a wicked stain.
For now his son is left to gain the father's legacy - now his aim.

The joy the pain the dreams all aged, yet their seasoned love remains.
The love unleashed to tame all fear would soon be faced with loves last tear,
For cancer's twisted ways unfold she leaves her son with pain to hold.

All is done but thoughts remain feeling powerless to constrain
Is this not the better life? No more darkness no more strife?
Could this be freedom's sting that sets them free to finally sing?

Singing, dancing and alive in grace
They fought the fight they finished the race.

Chad Spriggs originates from Northeast Texas. His debut album YOU OFFER ME was released January 2009. Chad is married to Deanna Spriggs, and they enjoy spending time with family, relaxing with friends, and challenging others to grow their relationships with God.

Debbie Stuckey

Beyond Me

SOMETIMES GOD IS beyond me. I can't understand where His sovereignty and man's will intersect. How can I comprehend the Trinity? Omniscience is far beyond my reason. Knowing my poverty, this mysterious God explains Himself by relating to my most intimate relationships—father/child and husband/wife. But even with that comparison, the greatness of His love for me is hard to believe. Is it possible that God could love me—this flawed child—with the same unconditional flood that I sometimes feel for my own children? Like that day with Rachel in first grade.

There you stood,
Shiny face framed by braids,
Flashing that beautiful smile I love to see.
Confident,
A little giggly,
And totally lovable.

A memory snapshot.

It was an ordinary, rush-to-school day.
Your sister applied her makeup on the way.
We almost forgot the lunches.
We were NOT early.

As you got out of the car,
With all the fumbling and grabbing,
You dropped your lunch box,
Shut the door,
Picked up the lunch box with a sheepish grin,
And said, "I love you,"
(Through the closed window.)

And then you just stood there—smiling.

For some stupid reason,
I thought I should be stern,
But you just kept standing there—smiling,
Until a smile forced itself upon me.

And all the time that you were smiling,
My heart was breaking,
And I knew afresh that I loved you,
Completely,
Passionately,
And forever.

As hard as it is for us to believe, His Word resounds with an unequivocal, "Yes!"

"I have loved you with an everlasting love."

—Jeremiah 31:3

Debbie Stuckey is a speech pathologist in western Arkansas. She and her husband Bill have three creative adult children who have grown and flown, but continue to feather the Stuckey nest with two wonderful in-laws and two precious grandchildren. She loves reading God's other book—His extravagant creation.

Sharon Paavola

GOD ANSWERS PRAYER

WHILE I SAT in the waiting room, my psychiatrist checked me into the mental hospital. I pleaded with God, "Please, Father, I'm desperate. I can't take it any longer. If you don't help me now, I don't want to live anymore. This is your last chance." I came in for a regular appointment but I needed to be hospitalized. I knew the depth of my depression and despair was more than I could handle on my own.

My doctor returned asking me to follow him. We went down a familiar hallway. But wait, he's going through different doors. What's this? Where's he taking me? A large open room with people staring confronted me. I realized I was locked in. I panicked. Why am I here? Emotionless, the staff informed me my stay would be 72 hours. Are they insane? I don't need to be in lock up. O Lord, what's going on? Did you hear my cry?

My thoughts ran wild. Time to calm down and assess how bad this really is. Oh no, there's a woman racing around putting chairs and tables in place. She continues to repeat her behavior. I don't belong with these people. They are disturbed and out of control.

Dinnertime now. I choked down a few bites. The "chair lady" is at it again. Oh, my, gosh, she's bare from the waist up. Shrieks pierce the air. The staff calms everyone down. I really don't belong here, can't you tell?

Now they want to process me and find a place for me to sleep. Please, just leave me alone! As they find a cot for me to lie down next to the nurses' station, my stomach revolts in gut wrenching pain. I think I'm going to die it hurts so bad. The "chair lady" comes by telling me she knows why my abdomen is bothering me. I must be pregnant. I yelled at her to go away barking at her that I couldn't be expecting since I'd had a hysterectomy when I was 27. Harsh words spilled out at her for disrupting my safety, making my aching worse. The staff moved me to a room with bunk beds where I clung to my purse and shoes afraid someone would steal them. I thought I might get some rest. An older woman in an adjoining room began yelling and ripping her bed apart. This went on for at least thirty minutes until the staff tied her down. That made her mad which caused her to scream incessantly hurting my ears. A nurse came with a sedative and I'm thinking at last, this will be the end of her for a while. She moaned forever prohibiting sleep for anyone. By the time rest came it was two or three in the morning. I woke up to chaos, startled at the reality of where I was. The nightmare hasn't gone away.

I put myself together as best I could for the interview with a woman who will evaluate whether I can leave lockup. We talked. I think she understood that I wasn't planning on killing myself today. She informed me that they would transfer me. I wanted to kiss her, hug her, and bring her flowers. I decided I could wait out the next hours as long as I didn't have to spend another night in lockup hell.

A staff member came over to give me my morning pills. A new pill was included with the regular ones. What's this? Oh, a medication my doctor wants me to begin taking. Oh, Lord are you answering my prayer? Did you hear me?

I settled in to watch a movie. I noticed someone motioning for me. It was time to leave lock up and go upstairs. Freedom! I knew God was beginning to heal me from the madness that afflicted me for the last twenty years! Now thirteen years later, that truly was the start of new joy in my heart.

Sharon Paavola speaks, writes, and encourages women to look to God for restoration, love, and forgiveness. With a deep background in biblical study and a full experience in her own life of God's redemption and mercy, her vulnerable approach touches hurting and broken lives.

Lisa Ragland

Celebrate Recovery

My HUSBAND AND I found out that our son was using drugs. In my heart I suspected it but had no proof until his friend showed up at our house one night, and I demanded the truth.

After our son graduated high school, he started to become someone we did not recognize. He was set to go into the Navy and at the last minute backed out. He decided he was suddenly not interested in college. Instead, he got a job and moved out on his own. We found out only a few short months later about his drug use.

We went to his apartment to confront him and take away his car. We then went home and did the only thing we knew to do - we prayed. That night I poured out my heartache and sorrows to God. I gave up control and asked God to intervene and help me accept whatever this course might take. In that moment, I had peace that passed understanding and fell sound asleep.

It didn't take long for God to show up. The next night my son was arrested. Even though this is the very thing we prayed for I needed God's strength to get through this. Out of love for our son we soon found ourselves making common parental mistakes that resulted in co-dependency.

At this time we changed churches, and we didn't yet have a support system. I made it a priority to continue my quiet time and Bible study. I just wanted to spend time with God.

A couple of months later, we had a night of crisis with our son. He came home in an uncontrollable rage after taking drugs. Afraid, I called the police. As a mom, that was a low point for me. The next morning we called our church and the pastor encouraged me to come right in even though he did not really know me. I was met with three wonderful people and lots of prayer and love. They were very concerned with what our son was going through but even more about how it might be affecting our whole family. They suggested that we attend Celebrate Recovery, one of the ministries of our church. That night my husband went, and after that the three of us started attending each week.

I thought we were going for our son, but I know now God was showing me that I needed to make some changes in my heart and actions. Celebrate Recovery is a 12-step Christ-based program which helps people not only deal with addictions, but with their own hurts, habits, and hang-ups. I realized I needed to work on issues of my own that were holding me back from the future that God had planned for me. The truths God showed me about myself were hard to face, but the more I went through the steps, the healthier I got emotionally and spiritually.

This is where the overflow of God's love happened. I finished my steps and went on to lead the teen girls group. God gave me love and empathy for what these girls faced because of the struggles my children faced in their teen years.

For me, my life is like putting together a puzzle. God does not show me how the pieces fit together but I have to trust Him with the whole picture. I know that trusting in Him all the time will get me through the tough times. I have used my experience to reach out to other parents going through the same tough season.

My husband and I rejoiced watching our son make wise choices. Unfortunately he recently fell back into destructive habits. While it is hard to stand back and watch my son live a life not honoring to God, I have hope in the promise that God is in control and that He loves my son.

Lisa Ragland is a leader in the Celebrate Recovery Ministry at her church, as well as a facilitator of women's Bible studies. She loves being Mike's wife, mom of three adult children, and "Memaw" to three precious grandchildren.

B.G. Nevitt

LOOK BEYOND THE MOMENT

I SAT DOWN and held the hand of a man with brain cancer. Tears streamed down his cheeks as he told me that something I recently said changed his life. He had listened to me speak and his heart and mind were stirred by the importance of his legacy. He was totally unaware on that day of the tragic medical news he was about to receive.

He sat in a tavern after that Sunday service, thinking about what he has just heard. He pushed aside the Bloody Mary in his hand. In that moment, he got up and walked out of that bar and said, "I don't want this to be the legacy I leave." His friends tried to convince him to stay but he was determined that his story needed a new ending.

It is exceedingly rare for someone to radically adjust the direction of his or her life before a painful crossroad event. Most of us wait for our lives to bottom out prior to reaching for something better. But when we catch a glimpse of something so wonderful and so attractive that it stirs our desires, something deep inside begins to dream of what could be.

The seeds of a dream have been planted in your life. They may have been forgotten; you might be tempted to think that impossibility has strangled any hope of reviving them. But take another look. The very thing that lies dormant may hold the power to transform your existence. That dream can stir your faith for the far greater plan God has prepared just for you.

A great dream will cause you to awaken in the morning with fresh energy and enthusiasm for that new day. When you have something wonderful to reach for, every day becomes an adventure and every opportunity becomes exciting.

But on the way to your dream, life happens. Problems and adversity will make every effort to derail you. That's why it's important to understand, God does not give you a dream to frustrate you. That dream is a gift from your heavenly Father to propel you toward your God-given destiny.

A few weeks ago, I was discouraged by words others had spoken into my life. My dream was wonderful, but I felt abandoned by those I thought were friends. I did not have the time, but a previously scheduled meeting required that I travel to Wyoming. During a moment of free time, I stood on the side of a mountain praying. I asked God to do something about my situation.

I looked at a dead tree surrounded by many large and healthy green trees. I studied that tree wondering what has caused it to die even though it was planted in such a wonderful environment. All the other trees were beautiful and thriving. Suddenly I felt the Lord speaking to me to stop staring at the dead tree. Stop focusing on death and look beyond.

I adjusted my line of sight past the tree. Off in the distance was another beautiful mountain range. Below the mountains was a beautiful lake and nearby a herd of elk grazed peacefully. I was so busy studying the dead tree I missed the beauty waiting to be enjoyed.

Suddenly a new perspective and determination became mine. I sensed my heavenly Father reminding me of the dream that burned in my heart. I was challenged to reactivate the very thing He has planted deep within me. I can no longer afford to be an expert on death and decay.

Opposition and adversities may attempt to wreak havoc, but you have the freedom to choose the direction of your focus. What God has planted in you is destined to flow through you. Look for life and spread words of life as seed for those around you.

I remembered my friend who pushed aside the Bloody Mary that represented his past. One week before he passed away we sat together in his front yard, there was a sense of anticipation for his new eternal adventure. With a twinkle in his eye he said, "I'm in His hands now! Just like him, I learned there is something greater that is worth reaching for. Seize the moment. It's not too late to reach.

BG Nevitt is the Lead Pastor of GT Church, a rapidly growing congregation in Central Illinois. This "Pistol Packing Preacher" serves as a sworn officer and chaplain for the Decatur Police Department. Married 33 years to his high school sweetheart, Brenda, he is the father of two daughters and grandfather of one. www.bgnevitt.com

Lyndie Blevins

When I Sing to Jesus

Before I knew the wonders of the cross
I was taught to sing of Jesus and His love for us all.
I sang those simple melodies loud and strong
'Cause when I sing to Jesus, His Spirit sings along.

As the years went by, His Spirit's voice was raised,
Weaving in my soul, those songs of love and praise.
Arranging melodies to graceful harmonies
'Cause when I came to Jesus, His Spirit sang to me.

And when the day is long, and I think I've lost my way,
Through the mist, I still hear His old tunes play--
Melodies of love bring me back to where I belong,
'Cause when I need a Savior, His Spirit starts the song.

The day I learned to raise my praise in song,
My life was changed forever, 'cause His Spirit sang along.

When I sing to Jesus, His Spirit sings with me,
His melodies of love are all the tune I need.
His harmonies of grace create the jubilee
'Cause when I sing to Jesus, His Spirit sings with me.

Lyndie Blevins lives in Duncanville, Texas, with two dogs, a cat, and occasional wildlife. She recently retired from a management career in information technology where she wrote policies and procedures. Lyndie is now embarking on a writing career. She teaches senior adult ladies in Sunday school.

Susan Titus Osborn

Loving Too Little, Loving Too Much

STARING OUT MY hotel window on that winter's day in Arlington, Virginia, I watched huge chunks of ice drift lazily down the Potomac River. In the cold stillness before me, I saw no boats, no children, and no birds. Huge chunks of ice impeded the flow of the mighty Potomac. I rubbed my arms and shivered—partly from the cold, but mostly from the memory forming in my mind.

I recalled the morning several years before when my husband, looking tired and tense, walked into the kitchen. He sat down at the breakfast table and said, "I care about you, but I don't love you enough to live with you anymore."

After twenty-two years of marriage, my world crumbled around me. I had suspected things weren't quite right between us, but I didn't dream that he wanted out of our marriage.

Going through a divorce in 1987 was the most painful ordeal I have ever experienced. I met my husband at seventeen and fell in love. We were married four years later. With the addition of two sons, our family life flowed smoothly like the Potomac River on a warm, summer day.

Then problems arose—easily solved at first, but more difficult to solve later on. It takes two to make a marriage work, and my husband was no longer willing to try. I built an icy wall of insulation around myself to keep from feeling the pain of his rejection. As time passed, I became numb from the cold. I forgot how to love; I forgot how to live. The course of my life became filled with chunks of ice like the Potomac River on that cold, wintry day.

Emotionally, I had been too stressed to pray and too fragmented to read the Bible. Like the river, I could no longer be an effective vessel for the Lord if my heart was ice-encrusted—if I was not capable of feeling.

I cried out, "Lord, I never dreamed the death of my marriage would be so painful. I don't ever want to be hurt like that again." I felt as useless as the cold river below me.

I stood at the window lost in thought for a long time. As winter passed, the sun would warm the river and bring it back to life again. The boats, the children, and the birds would return. I needed to let go of the icy wall in my heart, too. I needed to allow God's Son to warm me, to work in my heart and my life again.

Fast-forward to twenty years later. Once again I am standing in a hotel room, overlooking the mighty Potomac River. But this time, my second husband, Dick Osborn, is by my side. What a contrast! It is summer, and boats chart a course up and down the river, bringing tourists and cargo. Children fish and play on the river's wide banks. Geese, ducks, and heron dip into the lazy river to find food.

As I look back on the past twenty years, I realize that God has taught me valuable lessons. But His timing was not my timing. Instantaneous changes were my desire. I didn't like the position I was in, but I began to realize that God had placed me there for a reason. He used each painful situation to strengthen my faith and to help me grow. And God had provided. During the six years I was single, my oldest son, Richard, and I both graduated from college, and my youngest son, Mike, was well on his way. We never missed a meal or were unable to make a house payment. Yet, I realized these things were not accomplished solely by our own efforts. God was directing our paths every step of the way.

Loving too much leaves us open to the danger of being hurt, but loving too little can cause us to forget how to love and forget how to live. Once I learned to depend on God's strength, I found His love, presence, and peace in a way I had never known before.

Susan Titus Osborn is director of the Christian Communicator Manuscript Critique Service. She has authored 30 books. Susan is a member of the CLASSEMINARS staff and is a CLASS speaker. Susan lives in Fullerton, California, with her husband Dick. Susan can be reached at www.Christiancommunicator.com.

Shannon Chumadevsky

God Is Not Keeping Score

DO YOU BELIEVE that God keeps score? If He does, then do you get more points for certain things than others? Does He deduct points for sin, and add them back upon repentance? Until I experienced the overflow of God's love and grace this is how I would describe my Christian walk.

I grew up in a pastor's home with two parents who passionately loved God, and treasured me. If the church doors were open, we were there. As I got older, it sometimes felt that being a preacher's kid was a little like living in a fishbowl. People were watching me. I don't think that they were hoping I would stumble, but waiting to see if I would. I was determined not to.

Somewhere in my immature mind I had convinced myself that my poor choices would directly affect my parents. One wrong step and I would not only disappoint the two people that meant the most to me, but could taint the amazing ministry that they were pouring their lives into.

The performance had begun. I would never have considered myself a judgmental person but I was subconsciously taking note of others, and pondering, "What is she doing for the Lord that I'm not? Does He love her more than He loves me?" I heard some of the ladies in the church click their tongues in condemnation at lifestyle choices others were making. I was listening to the gossip, and slowly the margin for error began to narrow. I started playing by their rules.

I'm grateful my relationship with God was a constant in my life. I didn't even know what it felt like to not have him at the center of my world. I loved Him and so desperately wanted to please Him. I knew He loved me, however, somewhere deep down inside, I believed there was a point system. If I raised my hands during worship, point. If I listened to Christian music, point. If I read my Bible, point. Don't get me wrong these are all great things, but the line began to blur as to why I was doing them. I thought God was keeping score.

It was a dance I didn't even know I was doing. I was happy, felt like I had it all together. My childhood was storybook and my high school years were a dream. I guess I had made it through without ruining my life or my parent's reputation. Mission accomplished, right?

I became an adult and married my wonderful Christian husband, Jack, who had a point system mentality as well. Now we were dancing together. Six years into our marriage we moved into a major transition in life. We welcomed our son Chaise, sold our business, and moved from Seattle to Phoenix all in a six-month window of time. It was a season of uncertainty, but something had changed, the fishbowl had vanished. I was in a new city; I didn't know anyone there so I had no one to impress and no one knew me so suddenly there were no expectations to live up to. I can't put my finger on the precise moment it happened, I just know that at some point God poured his love and grace in heaping abundance over me. I was experiencing His overflow. I began to grasp from the bottom of my heart that His love for me was completely unconditional. He didn't love me more because of my lifetime pursuit to make wise choices. Wisdom was meant to guard my path, not to earn His love. Out of the overflow He forgave me for the pride of thinking I could hold it together in my own strength and the self- righteousness of believing I was doing it better than others around me. The comparisons stopped and the pressure was lifted; all of the "points" that I thought I had accumulated over the years began to blow away like leaves in an autumn wind. It was such a new and life altering glimpse into who God was. My understanding of His character began to expand. Why had it taken me so long to figure out that the God I adored wasn't petty? He was love, and I not only felt it, but found rest in it. What a relief to discover that the God of the universe was not in the box I had put Him in, holding my scorecards.

Shannon Chumadevsky feels blessed to have been given a heart that is moved by women who don't recognize their value or potential. Writing has been the avenue in which God is using her to connect, encourage, and inspire women to recognize how precious they are in His sight.

Tama Westman

ALONG CAME A PUP

THE LAST THING we needed was another mouth to feed. Our family had spiraled downward for years. Because Gary and I quit our jobs to put our son back together again after plowing through a windshield from the backseat of a friend's vehicle, we had our own vehicles repossessed, were in bankruptcy and about to lose our home to foreclosure. Unable to provide for his family, my husband was so depressed that one day he refused to get out of bed, saying he planned to lay there until he died. Only after I smashed a few dozen glasses against the kitchen door in utter frustration did he drag himself out of bed, give me a hug, and grab the broom.

Perfect timing for a new pup, right?

Let's get a puppy that will pee on the carpets, chew the doorknobs, dig holes in the yard and be a general nuisance and destructive force while we try to fix up the house, prepare for showings to potential buyers, and figure out our next step. But then, God's blessings sometimes don't seem like blessings at all.

A once loving, close, Christian family, steeped in our faith, we had somehow lost our way so completely, we were in danger of losing the one thing we had left, each other.

Along came a scruffy little brown-haired puppy, one who would grow to be 110 pounds and six-feet tall when standing on his hind legs. And with this pup, God poured out His love on us all. Cocoa Bear was so full of joy and astonishment at every little thing, one couldn't help but share in his happiness when he discovered an inch-worm, chased a butterfly, or watched the Canadian geese fly over head.

Cocoa taught us to smile again. As he dragged us on his leash, literally, down the path, through the woods, and around the lake, he showed us how to see the beauty and glory of God's world, as seen through his eyes. Cocoa didn't worry about finances and bills. He knew he would be fed each day and find a comfy bed by the fire each night. It didn't matter if we went for a car ride, for a walk, or just played fetch in the yard, as long as we were together, he was happy.

As we shared in Cocoa's joy, our hearts healed. Our lives mended.

Our perspective was changed, regardless of our circumstances. In the next few years, we would suffer more hardship and harrowing experiences, but the path to peace had already begun. God's love poured to us through the fount of love in that dog, and helped us find the strength and stamina we needed to not only survive, but surmount, our circumstances.

And then, with our hearts well on the mend, Cocoa had one more lesson for us. He taught us to grieve.

Diagnosed with the most vile, determined-to-destroy cancer, we tried several procedures, operations, and rounds of chemotherapy, bankrupting what resources we'd restored to save his life. Until we realized, he wasn't meant to live forever.

Cocoa Bear was a gift from God, purposely placed as a conduit of His love. He stole the ragged remnants of our hearts and returned them whole, able to profess the words of John 7:38, "He who believes in Me, as the Scripture has said, out of his heart will flow rivers of living water."

Now, I take my walks with Oreo, a scrappy Border Collie-mix determined to keep me young. But, as I look across the fields, I sometimes see the long flying tail, and slobbering smile from a big, brown mammoth bounding from one dune to the next. His dog tags jingling on the breeze, I faintly hear him call, "Look, Mom, a blue butterfly!"

Tama Westman is a freelance writer with over 1000 articles in print, including contributions to *Along the Way for Teens*, and *The Groovy Chicks' Road Trip to Love*. She is the Director of Communications for CLASSEMINARS, Inc., editor of the CLASS Communiqué, and co-owns A Write Start Communications—a company dedicated to helping writers.

Cheri Cowell

Breakfast on the Sea of Galilee

I FROZE. MY senses heightened; the Sea of Galilee spread out before me. From this rocky shore Jesus had shouted to the disciples, "Throw your nets on the other side of the boat."

For three days I'd traveled with a contingent of Christian journalists to some of Israel's holiest of sites. With every stop we made, I reached into the pages of the Bible and touched history. Less than twenty-four hours ago, the Author of that history touched me.

We'd left Masada, the winter palace of King Herod and before that we'd been in En Gedi and saw the caves where David secretly snipped the edge of Saul's robe. We were now traveling by escort through the militarized zone between Israel and Jordan to Kaser El Yehud, the site where Joshua led the children of Israel across the Jordan into the Promised Land. This is also the historic location on the Jordan River where John baptized Jesus. As the van bumbled along the dirt road past barbed wire with signs warning of land mines, my mind raced. I sensed God was speaking but I couldn't understand what He was saying. When the van stopped, we piled out—our military escorts, sporting AK47's, stood at a respectful distance. We walked down the mud-covered steps into the rushing waters of the Jordan. The moment I stepped into the water, the Holy Spirit overcame me. Swoosh! I nearly fell as my knees buckled; a warm current pulsated through my body taking my breath away. In my mind's eye I saw the descending dove and heard in my spirit the words, "In you I am well pleased." Tears poured as the reality of those words soaked my spirit. Although they were spoken more than 2000 years ago for His beloved Son whom John was baptizing in these waters, I now heard them spoken for me. My heavenly Father was pleased in *me*. Not because of anything I'd done or would do, but because I am His. There is nothing I could do, no mountain I could climb or desert I could cross, that would cause Him to love me more.

I must admit, I am a doer. I'm a take the situation by the driver's seat kind-of-gal, but my "doer" had just been snipped. It was a feeling I was unfamiliar with. In Bible studies I'd taught the difference between doing and being for God, but never had I experienced the *feeling* of not needing to "do."

In the following twenty-four hours I wrestled with my new reality. The next day, as we toured the ancient tels at Dan and Hazor and touched the ancient stones, a battle raged within me. *How am I to simply "be" without working to accomplish things for the Lord? What are you saying to me, God?*

The day was closing as I walked out of the Chapel of St. Peter's Primacy onto the shore of the Sea of Galilee, and it was happening again. However, this time, instead of the world closing in, it was opening up. All of my senses grew keen—the sound of the Galilean water lapping upon the rock-strewn shore floated through the air; a whisper of wind kissed my skin as it blew across the sea. And I almost smelled the fish frying as Jesus cooked breakfast. "It is the Lord," Peter cried out as he leapt from the boat. I felt a presence near me, like we do when someone familiar enters a room unaware. Then, as clearly as Peter had heard the words himself, I heard Jesus say to me, "Cheri, just feed my sheep."

I smiled and replied, "Yes, Lord, I can do that."

After the resurrection, Peter and the disciples had gone back to what they knew. They'd gone back to fishing, even after they'd been with the Risen Lord. I'd fallen into that same trap—simply going through the motions. Perhaps you have, too. We're dry, yet we continue to go through the motions of what we know how to do—passionless, without joy. Yet, just as Jesus said to Peter, He's saying to you and to me, "In you I am well pleased, so feed my sheep. Out of the abundance I'm giving you, go feed those who are hungry. Because you are loved *just because* you are Mine, go now and feed others with the overflow of what I'm pouring into you."

Cheri Cowell was blessed to be one of six Christian journalists chosen for an Israeli Ministry of Tourism sponsored tour of the Holy Land in November 2009. To see photos from her trip and to learn more about Cheri's writing and speaking ministry, visit her website www.CheriCowell.com

Carolyn Goss

LIVING WATER

SAME TO YOU, buddy!"

"Come on, you old geezer, move it!"

"Excuse me, can't you read? The sign says 'The line forms here!'"

Sound familiar? Certainly not because you, like me, have ever (ahem) muttered these words or anything like them! I'm always cognizant that I represent Jesus Christ!

Would that my assertion were true. Hard experience and a few self-surgeries in painfully extracting my foot from my mouth have taught me to be a little more careful than I used to be about "shooting from the hip" with my words, but being a naturally gregarious person who likes to fill up the conversational space, I have to do what Archie Bunker used to command his wife Edith to do: "Stifle myself." It isn't easy for me.

I grew up in a desert climate. I remember how thrilled we Stanford kids were when it rained. We would get little plastic boats and make dams in the curbs in front of our house.

Playing in water was a rare treat for us, but for farmers, ranchers, miners, loggers, and other skilled laborers, water was a necessity. Because collecting precious water from mountain snow melt and runoffs was the only viable way to have enough water to support the settlers who moved there in the days before air conditioning, water reclamation became a major area of study long before I was even born.

When our youngest son used to ask me a question about a moral or ethical issue, I tended to launch into a "Let me teach you everything I know about the pros and cons of the subject" answer. After a couple times of seeing him roll his eyes and announce, "I feel a lecture coming on," I realized that dumping the stores of my vast wisdom into his psyche wasn't the way to respond. I cannot say I always listened first and then weighed my words before answering, but I knew it was the right thing to do.

I knew, and know, that Jesus would respond to a seeker's questions in the way that best met the inquirer's needs. His words did not flow like a tsunami that is oblivious about leaving damage and destruction behind it. Rather, they flowed like a brook of clear, sun-kissed, life-giving water there for the taking for people who desire to fill their thirsty souls with it. I am a follower of Jesus and I want to model my interactions with people after His, not just in words but in actions. I want some of that water. So where to begin? Jesus tells us. "For out of the overflow of the heart the mouth speaks."

There it is—the water metaphor Jesus so often uses. ". . .out of His being will flow living water. . ."

John 7:38-39 Psalm 36:8 John 4:16-19

Carolyn Goss is a professional writing coach and book editor, freelance copyeditor, book doctor, and ghostwriter. She and her husband Len cowrote *Little Style Guide to Christian Writing and Publishing*. Carolyn and Len are partners in life and in goodeditors.com.

Evelyn W. Davison

LIVING FREELY IN LOVE'S OVERFLOW

DURING THE GREAT Depression six-year-old Johnny lived with his grandmother while his dad served in the Army Air Corps. He believed God answered prayer. After a long day, Granny tucked him in and listened to his prayers — three times— before she settled down to read her Bible and pray. Hearing him get out of bed again, she listened and heard him praying loudly, "Lord, I want a bicycle for my birthday so I can be free to go and do things. Would you give Granny some money and tell her to get me one! She will believe you, but remember to open her ears first. She is really hard of hearing. Thanks! Amen."

Granny cried herself to sleep that night as she prayed for Johnny and America.

In January 1941, President Franklin D. Roosevelt gave his State of the Union Address to Congress. The world was shaking in fear of a young charismatic leader named Adolph Hitler.

Roosevelt spoke with a troubled heart about four freedoms that could bring hope and change the world. They were: Freedom of Worship, Freedom of Speech, Freedom from Fear, and Freedom from Want. The last two freedoms, which went beyond America's Constitution and protected by its First Amendment, became America's cry to the world to rise up and fight for freedom.

We remember Roosevelt best for, "The only thing we have to fear is fear itself."

In the height of that time of terror, Norman Rockwell did a series of freedom paintings, which became covers for *The Saturday Evening Post* in 1943.

The most famous was not "Freedom from Fear," but "Freedom from Want." This painting of a happy family around their Thanksgiving table focusing on Grandpa and a turkey depicted America's blessings and God's abundance. It set hearts to dreaming.

God's Word gives us a better concept of thankfulness and what it means to have freedom to live in love's overflow. "I know what it is to be in need, and I know what it is to have plenty. I have learned the secret of being content in any and every situation, whether well-fed or hungry, whether living in plenty or in want. I can do everything through Him who gives me strength" (Philippians 4:12-13).

Paul did not say we can have everything. He said we can do everything! How can that be in a time such as this today when everything we hold precious is being broken or stolen? Maybe a lesson from a child can answer that question.

A Sunday school teacher asked kindergarteners who could quote the 23rd Psalm. Christina was first to raise both hands. She jumped up, faced the class, and said, "I am a little sheep and the Lord is my shepherd. I just want to be like Him so I'm just following him around." She bowed sweetly and sat down.

Christina is right on! The Lord is our Great Shepherd and our Provider. He has a four-step program for living in the overflow:

- Be joyful — Happiness is a choice, while joy is a gift.
- Pray continually — God's phone number is Jeremiah 33:3, "Call me and I will answer you."
- Give thanks — Thanksgiving births thanksliving.
- Live in Christ's strength — The Power of His Presence is greater than anything that can come against us (1 Thessalonians 5:16:18).

America has changed a lot since the Great Depression, and each day brings more reasons to live in fear. God has not changed, and His Word is true in good times and bad times. He says, "Blessed is the nation whose God is the Lord" Psalm 33:12.

Jesus is our Rope of Hope if we trust him, call on him, and seek to be like him. It is time for us to pray for such a time as this.

Yet, it doesn't hurt to call on Granny too! Especially, if she knows how to pray!

God's overflow of love, gift wrapped in mercy and grace, is available. Remember to ask for it! It is what America needs.

Evelyn Davison is affectionately known as The Love Lady. Evelyn devotes her life to helping others live freely in God's love. Evelyn can be reached at lovetalknetwork.com or evelyndavison@gmail.com.

Ron Benson

PLOWING GROUND

WE PLAYED SKIPBO on the deck while Dad persevered through the last day of his life. Good times.

Mom and Dad moved into our home in September of that year, and by June mini-strokes had slowly robbed my father of most of his abilities. Later that month, a severe stroke landed him in the hospital, followed by hospice care at the house.

Our family gathered to be with Dad. We situated his bed just inside the deck, accessing the summer sun and warm air. He was in the last hours of a long, productive, godly life—Jesus was calling him home. It didn't seem like an overflow moment, but fruit was all around.

Jesus' words about good fruit in Luke 6 imply that abundance "to overflowing" is a characteristic of fruit God produces. God is the master horticulturalist, a farmer of great skill and expertise. When God is allowed to do the farming, he always produces good fruit.

Isaiah describes God's farming efforts with these rhetorical questions:

> When a farmer plows for planting, does he plow continually?
> Does he keep on breaking up and working the soil?
> When he has leveled the surface,
> does he not sow caraway and scatter cumin?
> Does he not plant wheat in its place,
> barley in its plot,
> and spelt in its field?
>
> —Isaiah 28:24-26

God does not plow forever. My father had lived a long life, and God's plowing paid dividends in good fruit. Around the table that day on a pleasant summer evening, the family played cards while Dad lay breathing his last. We laughed and cried and celebrated within earshot just outside his door. While some of the fruit of God's work in his life dealt the next hand of Skipbo, Dad could hear the sounds of his family through the screen door.

Death is a robber and a thief, and God doesn't like it. But death—at least the fleshy kind—inevitably comes round and claims us. The knowledge of life lived in this world by faith, and of life after death in heaven, does not take away the loss, but it does take away the sting. How does God do that? What kind of painkiller does God use?

Some of the anesthesia God uses to cushion the pain comes directly from the fruit he has produced. Choosing to taste and enjoy and digest that fruit allows the pain of death and loss to be ameliorated, softened, and dulled by God's grace and love.

Sitting around the table, our family was the cumin, the caraway, the wheat. What God planted in the well-plowed soil of my father's life had sprung up, and provided proof that as a farmer, God knows what he is doing.

> All this also comes from the Lord Almighty,
> whose plan is wonderful,
> whose wisdom is magnificent.
>
> —Isaiah 28:29

Ron Benson has been a pastor for almost thirty years. Ron's articles have appeared in Today's Christian, Discipleship Journal, and Plain Truth Magazine, among other publications. With Coach Mike Gottfried, Ron authored the book *Coach's Challenge: Faith, Football, and Filling the Father Gap,* (Howard Publishing, 2007). Find Ron at www.ronbenson.net

Cindi Vana

God Bag

IN THE MIDST of a thousand believers, my head was only half listening. My body was in one place, my heart in another. My precious life-long friend was preparing to pack her bag for heaven. Breaking through, the speaker's words overcame my wandering thoughts. A God Bag? In the banquet hall, a brown bag and child's red crayon lay before me. I recognized His gentle tug, the God who touches and overflows our souls.

The speaker shared the story of a grizzled sheriff. An alcoholic, the sheriff abandoned his family to a job that took more than it gave. Alone in an alleyway, he longed for the bottle but longed more for love and life. Wiping tears from a weary face, the sheriff cried out to God and in that moment his cruiser became God's transport to grace. He looked for something, anything to capture the desperation of his heart. All he found was a used crumpled lunch bag. Compelled to give every concern to Christ, he grabbed a colored marker and wrote - God Bag. Hardly able to write through his tears, he scribbled on scraps his hopes and prayers. On one wrapper he wrote—alcohol. Another named his wife. A torn napkin held the names of his children.

Decades passed, the worn bag rested prominently on his desk, a testament to a faithful God. The bag that years before had overflowed with hopelessness remained as a reminder of restoration. Curious visitors could not resist asking about the God Bag. Confident, the sheriff shared all that the bag represented in his earlier life—now a lasting legacy to God.

"You know," he said "for years my God Bag overflowed with prayers of desperation. It's taken a life to understand that my bag is now filled with praise not only prayers. That bag now overflows with praise for all that God has done in my life."

The speaker finished the sheriff's story. I hurried away, my own God Bag in hand. Immediately a call came with sad news, come within the hour. What did I have left to say to this forever friend? She walked a path I knew nothing about. I prayed, "Please God, bring your promise to this suffering situation."

Up the steps and through the door, like a hundred times before I entered. In the doorway, the sounds of life pulled at my heart. The house hummed with family and grandchildren. Still, I heard the hush of a coming end.

I held back in the hallway, I wanted to see my friend but not like this. She called to me "Why are you hanging back? I need to talk to you." I watched my friend struggle from her living room bed. My feet anchored in the hallway by fear, she lumbered toward me. Steadied by a faithful husband's arm, she asked "What do you do when God decides not to answer your prayer?"

I clinched my fist, God Bag in hand. Then, out of the overflow of God's grace came His response for their hearts. I began to tell them of the God Bag. Words began to flow from a bigger heart than my own, "Even as you pack your God Bag for heaven, we first unpack every earthly care. We take only the treasures of heaven with us and leave our baggage behind. This is your time to praise Him for every answered prayer. Your treasures are the overflow of your life—God's answered prayers, too many to recount."

In our lives there are times when asking is not nearly as important as praising. When we persist in only asking, we risk being blown off course. Praise keeps us on course with God. Praise is our pathway to promise and our footpath of faith. When we find ourselves living on the edge of despair it is time to visit our God Bag—to unpack every answered prayer and praise Him for a life lived out of His overflow.

My friends stood there, hearing the fresh hope of God. The place of petition was no longer sufficient for the days ahead. Serenity settled across their faces, "We can do that!" they proclaimed. "What joy it will be to spend these last hours packing our God Bags with praise, the overflow of God's goodness and grace."

Cindi Vana is an experienced broadcast communicator on LoveTalk Christian radio. Ministering globally, she consistently challenges the myths of culture with the message of Christianity. Passionate about prayer, she serves as Texas State Coordinator of National Day of Prayer—mobilizing millions to pray daily for our nation. LoveTalknetwork.com

Debra Brown

THE PURCHASE

I SHOVED THE Spiderman action figure back on the shelf. A picture of all the Spiderman dolls lying in my grandson's toy box flashed through my mind. I paced aisle after aisle of the toy store, looking at the same toys in the last three stores. Grabbing my cell, I phoned a friend.

"Denise, help. Carter's birthday is in forty-five minutes. Do you have any suggestions for the best gift ever?"

"Have you thought about LeapFrog? My boys love it."

Yes, Carter loved computer games. In fact, we discovered them together. It was perfect. I could hear him plead, "Mams, when Coen takes his nap, can we play on the computer, please?"

Rushing to the LeapFrog aisle, I snagged the most expensive kit, and headed for the checkout counter. The ticking clock reverberated in my ears, drowning out the sale of the day announcement.

Back in the car, I glanced over at the perfect purchase lying on the front seat. My shoulders slumped, it was a dismal reflection of the extravagant love my husband and I felt for our grandson. Is it wrong to want to lavishly bless my grandchildren?

I knew the answer.

1 John 3:1 ran through my mind: "How great is the love the Father has lavished on us, that we should be called children of God."

The tires crunching on gravel diverted my thoughts, as I made the final turn into the park. Children's laughter filled the air and balloons hovered over party tables; the same tables Carter and I run past as we scale castle walls and defeat dragons on our many Wednesdays together. I reached for my package, and headed for the picnic tables.

"Mams, Mams, you're here."

Two small hands wrapped around my waist, hugged me tight and were gone. Oh, the bliss!

"That's my Mams," Carter said to his friends, "we play here together a lot.

The package in my hand was lifeless, but the overflow of love came from my relationship with Carter.

I brought the perfect gift to the party. It was not my purchase. It was me.

I showed up, and with me, I brought a promise of overflow of more days of discovery together.

"Mams, let's play LeapFrog."

Two hands, one wrinkled and one very small, intertwined around the LeapFrog game. Laughter spills over the room.

"Hit the right button, Carter, now the left. You did it. Good job."

Next year will bring another birthday, and I'll have to find another purchase, but I'll never have to find another perfect gift.

Debra Brown and her husband Jim have two married daughters and four grandchildren Debra has been working with children for over thirty-five years: Teaching, leading worship, writing curriculum, directing drama, and musical productions. She loves worshipping the Lord, her family, and writing children's stories with her daughters.

Doreen Hanna

God's Promise of Hope

IT WAS JULY of 2002. Chad, my husband of 25 years, had just entered a men's recovery home to overcome his alcohol addiction. His good decision required us to move out of our home and place all of our belongings in storage because we could not carry the lease on our home and also pay for the funds required for him to live at the "Gratitude Retreat." Our youngest daughter and her husband invited me to come and stay with them for the next six months Chad would be away.

Within three days after this life impacting change in my life I was faced with a decision the morning of the Anaheim, CA, Christian Booksellers Convention. Was I going to attend? This would be the first time for me to submit my curriculum proposal to publishing house editors. It was my secret hope that Focus on the Family would be there, because that is who I really desired to publish my curriculum. I had already been feeling nervous, but now I felt downright fearful, doubting my work, and my self-worth. My emotions were overflowing. I thought to myself, "Can I muster the courage to present my curriculum proposal when I felt like my life was in shambles?"

With that question rambling loudly in my mind I suddenly felt prompted to just pull on the reins of my emotions, shoot up a prayer, and head out the door to CBA. I swiftly drove down the 405 Freeway, before I lost my nerve. Suddenly a verse that had spoken to me several times recently came to mind, "I know the plans I have for you, plans for good and not for evil to give you a hope and a future" (Jeremiah 29:11).

Upon my arrival Linda Jewell was waiting for me at the front door of the convention center. We sat down together and she reviewed my curriculum. Her first words to me were, "Oh Doreen, this is wonderful, I know you are going to get published!" Between God and Linda I was greatly encouraged and walked into CBA with excitement.

That day several editors asked for my proposal. I was thrilled. Within days I had submitted my proposal to the appropriate publishing houses. Then, within 60 days each of them sent me their rejection letters.

Those rejections seemed to become a way of life for the next five years. I had received 12 rejections but continued to self-publish, because I saw God at work through this ministry and I was not giving up on my secret desire to see Focus on the Family publish my curriculum.

By 2006 I secured a publishing agent. After a year of submitting the curriculum to other publishers with no results, he recommended I write a book about why our American Christian society needed this rite-of-passage that enabled teen girls to see themselves as true Modern Day Princesses, Daughters of the King.

I was passionate to have others hear and ultimately experience the value of this ministry so I said, "I'll do it." Upon completion of a book proposal I also had the joy of having Pam Farrel, a wonderful woman and seasoned author, come alongside of me as my co-author.

In October 2007, at the Glorieta Writers Conference, I was thrilled to hear that Focus on the Family was on site. Soon I was sitting across the table from one of their senior editors. She embraced the proposal immediately, the Acquisitions Committee soon said, "Yes," and FOTF offered us a contract by February 2008.

January 2010, our book, *Raising a Modern Day Princess*, and the Becoming a Modern Day journal (the curriculum!) was released.

OH! Chad too has been released - from the bonds of alcoholism. He has been sober for more than eight years!

My heart still overflows with joy when I think of God's promise of hope that He gave me that day years ago and how that promise is nestled in my heart for eternity.

I pray it overflows into your life—today!

Doreen Hanna is a speaker and writer living in Santa Fe, NM and founder of Treasured Celebrations ministries. www.doreenhanna.org

Vicki Draeger

Heart Song

My spirit soars at the magnificence of Your creation.
    My body trembles before the power of Your will.
"Let there be," is all You said,
    and there was. . .
Your voice brought forth majestic mountains,
    verdant forests, vast oceans, infinite stars. . . and us.

Formed in Your image, designed for love, for relationship
    You gave us the world, but we sought our own power.
Though made of clay, we were not pliant.
    With hardened hearts we sank into sin and pursuit of pleasure.
Poor stewards of planet earth, our little garden
    Poor stewards of our selves, our very souls
Grief-filled, hopeless, wandering in a wilderness of loss and lust
    We did thirst for love, for relationship.

Out of the overflow of Your compassion, You sent a Savior
Out of the abundance of Your grace, You sent Your Son
    We reach for You,
        knowing that if we can but touch the hem of Your garment
            we can be healed, forgiven, redeemed.
    We can return to love, to relationship.

The floodgates of heaven burst forth and Your love drenches us
    in hope, in comfort, in joy.
Boundless love streams from You as
    we open ourselves to relationship.
Our cups runneth over with blessings
    And in the overflow we love and bless one another.
    We treasure and preserve Your creation.
    We perpetuate righteousness.
    For this, my heart sings.

Vicki Draeger, Ph.D. is mother of five, proud grandmother of one. From Hawaii, she founded Clearview Christian Girls' School as part of her ministry to women and children. She's education director for Keiki O Ka Aina, a Native Hawaiian agency. Published works include *The Vegetable Storybook for Readers and Eaters,* and *Kids, Quarks, and Quanta.* She can be reached at vickid43@yahoo.com

John Van Diest

PROJECT CHRISTIAN BRIDGE

JOHN, WOULD YOU be willing to go to Moscow and represent the association at the Moscow International Book Fair?" Doug Ross, president of the Evangelical Christian Publishers Association asked. It was 1983, and the cold war battled on. After thought and prayer I called Doug back and said yes.

As part of a nineteen person delegation we called *Project Christian Bridge,* President Mikhail Gorbachev met with us. His greeting, "You can't tell the Russians from the Americans," encouraged us in our efforts to create understanding and cooperation between American Christians and the USSR, Russia, and Ukraine.

At the time, Bibles were banned in their countries, but were also the hottest ticket in the black market. For seven days, thousands of people poured into a tiny, ten foot square booth so they could view our Christian books and Bibles. So hungry were these people for a taste of God's Word, that when I told a man the Bible boxes under our table were empty, he said, "May I have one so it will remind me of the Bible?" He begged for a scrap of God's spirit and it drove me to tears.

Most people wanted to hold a Bible and many wanted to buy one. When a woman asked, "Could I have a Bible?" my KGB "helper" answered, "Nyet." She scolded me, "Then why are you here?" The question haunted me for years, "How can we get more Bibles to them?"

For the next fair, we decided to ship 15,000 Bibles and see what happened. To our surprise, when we arrived at the booth, hundreds of cases waited for us. The KGB authorities called us into a special room and wanted to know, "How did you get these Bibles here?" Our answer, "We simply put labels on each box with the words "Moscow International Book Fair" and the proper booth number."

Word of the Bibles spread fast, and as a result, we were interviewed for the Moscow evening news and announced free Bibles at our booth the next day. The quarter-mile line was thick with grateful people. They snaked through the convention center and down the path outside for several blocks. An angry Madeline O'Hare expressed her frustration that the group circled by her own booth.

Through the years, our opportunities for ministry increased on a national and personal level. We were invited to spend an entire week as guests on the highest clearance level.

One of our most startling meetings took place with KGB leadership. The second in command courageously stated, "Many of us carry a lot of guilt for what we have done in the KGB over the last seventy years." One of our delegates responded, "I, too, carried a lot of guilt. But as a result of an encounter with Jesus Christ, He relieved me. And I would like to suggest that He can relieve you of the guilt you may be carrying." The general's eyes instantly filled with tears.

The emotion intensified when Alex Leonavich, another member of our team, shared how his family left Russia when he was only nine years old. One uncle was forced to stay behind and disappeared in Siberia. "I also hated the KGB and never forgave them for what was done to my uncle. But tonight, just as Jesus Christ forgave me of my sins, I would like to forgive you for what the KGB did to my uncle."

Warm hugs ended our time together. The general said, "I've only cried twice in my life, once, when my mother died, and then tonight."

We will never know how God's overflow touched the lives of those He supernaturally introduced to His Word. A whole generation has now been exposed to scripture and a Savior who offered sad, frightened people hope.

In 1992, ten men were chosen as guests of President Gorbechev to visit Russia and discuss the possible effect Christianity might have if incorporated into their society. Once again, I was honored to go. We were assigned government leaders and allowed open discussions about our faith.

Only a few years ago, the hungry people of the Soviet Union could not legally get their hands on a single Bible. Yet, a small group calling themselves *Project Christian Bridge* invested prayer, time, and money in answer to God's call. As a result, today, thousands of Christian books and Bibles roll off the presses in Soviet publishing houses. A spiritual feast of God's Word is theirs for the taking.

John Van Diest is an Associate Publisher at Tyndale House Publishers. Besides being the founding publisher of Multnomah and Vision House publishers, John has over a dozen books credited to his authorship. John has championed Christian publishing in many foreign countries.

Elaine Bowden

FREED TO OVERFLOW

"JOURNAL. IT WILL help your depression," my Christian psychiatrist advised me. No words would come for several years. Then they came so slowly, so fearfully, reluctantly gaining momentum. Finding "bringing every thought into captivity to the obedience of Christ," (NKJV 2 Cor 10:5b) gave spiritual credibility to the advice. My thoughts had never been credible to me, maybe Jesus would clarify them.

The words were halting and disorganized. One day the thought of writing my prayers in a blank book crossed my mind. Capturing my prayer-thoughts turned my thoughts into sentences and were very revealing. All sorts of things gushed out in relief, filling every page of the book. My trust in the Father growing. The need then seemed satisfied and I went on to other writing but my prayer life would never be the same.

As I studied, a Bible verse stuck in my head. Meditating on it was not enough, it wouldn't leave my mind until I captured the meditation on paper. Some emotion, some idea shifted as the words could be returned to paper. It became fun and when the verse seemed satisfied with my efforts, I was free to roam scripture again, until another verse would catch my attention. Pages and pages of verses spoke directly to my depression, giving reason for penning them on paper. Scripture had become alive and some verses became special.

Proverbs 13:12 spoke volumes, "Hope deferred makes the heart sick," (NASU). As a person who defers a lot to others, hope can get very tattered when left dangling. Add to that, the word hope in Hebrew is not the wishful thinking as it is in English today but means expectation. When expectations are deferred there is slow betrayal of trust and the heart is affected. It helped to know this. Could my responses to others be different or my expectations?

It was the rest of the verse that eventually revealed something much deeper. *But desire fulfilled is a tree of life.* Slowly, it came to me that I did not believe it was right for me to have desires. What I really did believe and operated under a piece of another verse - "I shall not want" (Psalm 23:1b). It was wrong to want, desire. In my mind, desire was proof of selfishness.

Later, "Delight yourself in the Lord and he will give you the desires of your heart." (NIV Psalm 37:4) would help. I decided to delight in the Lord would be a safe desire. That decision led me down a path that took me to heights of delight and joy I'd never known with the Lord. Then more scripture dealt with my sorrow too because they are connected to joy (Jeremiah 31:13, 2 Corinthians 7:7, James 4:9). Fear of misunderstanding scripture dissolved, and confidence grew.

The captivated words freed Christ, the Word, to reconcile my journey through depression. When I started thanking God for it (Philippians 4:7), Jesus began to reveal himself to me in a new way every time I went down. It had become the best thing that had ever happened to me. I related to Paul and his "thorn in the flesh" (2 Corinthians 12:8) that God would not take away, for in time I would find that depression was not going to go away. Like Paul I learned His grace is indeed sufficient.

His preciousness to me is in direct relationship to every deep depression. In my dark days, He is the Word and I listen. When I fail, He forgives and restores. It is such a wonderful compensation and I am content with the depression. I don't like the feelings of it, but the result is worth the pain.

One day studying Philippians 4:12a ("I know both how to be abased, and I know how to abound") (KJV), finding the meaning of these old English words in a Greek dictionary, was a shock. "Abased" means depressed or pressed down, and "abound" means to overflow. I had indeed learned to be content with depression. Now I was learning to overflow? The two were connected through learning to be content? God doesn't waste the negative but uses it to produce the positive? The idea, when captured to examine, was so comforting, so freeing.

Questions keep coming and the Lord reveals himself through the words. The Word himself becomes more alive through the words. Reconciliation is the result. Who knew, through depression I would be freed to overflow?

Elaine Bowden, writer, photographer, artist. Also a wife, mother, and grandmother. She writes to express the love God has shown her, his hope, his peace, his joy as well as the contrasts to the other things he also gives us, discipline, correction, and guidance through deep valleys. elainebowden@frontier.net

Dianne Guthmuller

A Plan for the Pain

A SLEEPLESS NIGHT turned to day. My eyes were swollen so much from crying through the night, I could hardly see. As the kids got ready for school, I wondered how I would face them. How would I hold it together? Leaning on the wall, I slowly moved down the stairs. It was as if I had become a bystander of my own life, watching the pain of the day unfold.

What would happen to my children and me? How would we survive? What about God's calling on my life? What about my dream?

One month after attending the CLASSeminar, my marriage of 22 years dissolved. I would never meet that goal of being a Christian wife and mother who protected her children from the pain of divorce. My marriage, my family, my ministry, my goals, and my dreams were changed forever. It was like I was a piece of pottery that was almost finished and then the potter suddenly changed his mind:

> Here I am; high upon this shelf…isolated…lonely…
> How long have I been here? Days, weeks, maybe months.
> I've lost track of time…I don't like it here…I'm so bored.
> But, it's much better than the other places I've been.
> First, there was the wheel…Round and round and round and round.
> The Potter's thumbs were constantly pushing and probing…
> One time He almost crushed me. I don't even feel like myself…
> Who am I? … What am I? … Where am I? …Oh…I'm so tired.
> Then there was the fire…No! No! Not that! What did I do? What did I say?

I'm sorry… I'll be good… I'm sorry I didn't turn out the way You planned…
Please, oh please don't destroy me.
Why are You so mad at me?
Pushing me… crushing me… burning me alive…
Is there anything left?
What do I look like?
Now, You're ignoring me…how long has it been?
It's a long way down. It's so high on this top shelf… I'm afraid…
I think the Potter is disappointed in the way I turned out…
What if He forgets about me?
I guess He's decided to use me to balance this shelf.
Wait! He's coming this way… He's looking at me… staring at me… He's smiling…
He's reaching out His hands for me…
Where am I going? I don't know… I don't care…
I'm in the Potter's Hands.

Many years have passed since the pain of my heart spilled onto a scratch piece of notebook paper. Today the pain and heartache reflected in this poem are no more than a faint memory, but the faithfulness, supernatural strength, and provision of my God are as fresh on my mind as if it were yesterday.

As I sit in my favorite chair with my first cup of coffee and plan the menu for Thanksgiving Day, my eyes glance at our latest family picture. Excitement will fill this house in a couple of weeks—five children and spouses and ten grandchildren! I can't help but remember that morning many years ago when I could barely make it down the stairs. Some days I still feel like an unshaped lump of clay, but it's okay…I'm in the Potter's Hands.

Dianne Guthmuller is an inspirational speaker and writer who utilizes her life experiences to encourage others and motivate them to change and grow. God's Word has been Dianne's compass, calm, and comfort during the happiest and hardest of times. Dianne and her husband Harry live in Northwest Florida and have five children and ten grandchildren. dianneguthmuller.com

Vicki Jantzen

First-Rate Help Mate

"The Lord God said, 'It is not good that the man should be alone; I will make him a helper fit for him.'"

—Genesis 2:18 (ESV)

AS A RECENTLY turned nineteen-year old, I said "Yes" to a proposal that my husband affectionately calls a 'two-fer'—"Will you be my wife and come to Colombia to live in the jungle with me?"

That was the start of more than sixteen years of adventure with a lifestyle that could have made a feature article in *National Geographic*, or the setting for a "Survivor" show. It was reality versus the imagined romantic Tarzan and Jane adventure I had in mind. Our lifestyle was rustic to say the least. We lived along a river in the jungle in bamboo houses with no electricity, no running water, cooking over wood fires, and washing clothes on a raft in the river. My children were birthed there, and I became not only Mom to them, but their teacher, too. We lived in the middle of a sector that was surrounded by terrorists, called 'guerrillas,' rebelling against the government, and Mafia cartels who were supplying arms and funding their activities through the drug trade. We saw white powder traded in the river store for refrigerators, boat motors, and sewing machines.

During those sixteen years, I was known as Dalton's wife, and later as Jesse, Seth, and Amy's mom, but who was I? What was my identity? Did helping my husband fulfill his call minimize who I was or was supposed to be?

I left the States as a teen bride, and returned as mother of a family with three children. Reintegrating to life in the United States was not that easy. Finding our place with no history as a couple or family meant we couldn't even get our own electricity or telephone or buy a car without a co-signer. I felt my identity growing more obscure. I had made a commitment the day we married, but did that mean I would be erased as a person?

Fast forward to a recent adventure as empty nesters. This time, our new facet of ministry was the creation of a ministry to pastors, missionaries, and Christian leaders called The Rekindling. One aspect of the ministry involved operating a retreat center, where I found myself in an important role as the retreat hostess. I cooked, washed, and cleaned for our retreat guests and served as the face of the ministry to the public—not glamorous, but important; appreciated, but not fulfilling.

Is this who I am, who I'm supposed to be? What about my dreams? What about my passions to teach, coach, and write? My questions weren't rooted in rebellion, but rather God stirring a hunger for the release of those talents while preparing me for the next adventure with Him.

Fast forward to today. The demands of operating a retreat center no longer consume our time and energy, and my husband and I are able to focus on what more completely fulfills our passion in ministry. I have found that God has given me dreams that support, help, and complement what He wants my husband and I to do together, rather than competing to see who has the more valid ministry direction.

Through this process, I've come to learn the value of what our friends Dawn and Dave Lind describe as a "Team of Two"—two hearts, two dreams blended into one, complementing each other and bringing a vital part to its fulfillment.

Learning that I'm part of a team with my husband helped me realize that what I do is important, integral, and part of the ministry, and it doesn't take away from who I am. I've developed into a multi-faceted person who is willing to do whatever God puts in my hand to do according to the best of my ability, and unto Him.

Along the way, I've found fulfillment and joy in knowing that I am an equal part of the team, not second-rate, but first-rate. There is room for me to hear from God and contribute. I have value. I have a place, because God put us together not for one of us to disappear, or to consume the other. Rather, He put us together to co-labor in the fulfilling of His dream for our lives.

Vicki Jantzen and her husband Dalton work as a "Team of Two" ministering to pastors, missionaries, and Christian leaders. Her experience as a missionary and lay pastor's wife gives her compassion for those they minister to in North and South America, and Southeast Asia through 30 60 100 Ministries, Inc.

Gary Chevalier

THE AROMA OF THE FAST

WHAT ARE WE going to eat for dinner tonight?" A common question around our household and yours, I suspect. Most every day my two daughters inquire about the evening cuisine, hoping they'll find out Mom is preparing one of their favorites like tacos or shrimp scampi. I get caught up in the anticipation of the evening meal! I love the smell of food as it is cooked; I love the blending of aromas as the separate courses rest together on the plate; and I love the rush of flavor that cascades through my mouth when I take that first bite. In my household, if it isn't the kids who are asking "What's for dinner," it's me. Simply put, I love to eat good food.

The irony in this is that a few Octobers ago, our church staff felt called to lead the church into a year of prayer and fasting. Moreover, in our role as pastors, we believed we were to set an example by starting the new year off with a 40-day fast. From January 1st to February 9th, we committed to sacrifice food to the Lord, asking Him to grow our church and use us in a mighty way.

The beginning of those 40 days went much as I, and probably you, imagined. I knew what it meant to be truly hungry. My body was in full rebellion, and by the third day of the fast, the thought of eating consumed me. (You don't really realize how many commercials on TV advertise grocery stores, restaurants, or other parts of food industry until you go without eating for a few days!)

Every aroma of food became a luxurious perfume, and it seemed that everyone I knew was asking me to go out to lunch (their treat, of course). It wasn't a picnic for my family either. Knowing my hunger, they felt awkward eating in front of me, around me, or even having food in the house that I enjoyed.

I still remember the tension and visible discomfort on my wife's face the first time we went out to eat together during the fast. After an exhausting day of work and shopping, my family landed at Chick-Fil-A for dinner. At first, my kids asked questions like, "Aren't you hungry, Daddy?" My wife refused to eat her meal, but eventually I coaxed her to eat as I sat beside them drinking a glass of fresh-squeezed lemonade. I became overwhelmed by God's peace and His presence during that (and subsequent) meals with them. As hungry as my body was, the desire to fill it with food became replaced with a desire to fill it with God. In the days that followed, the awkwardness of eating together with my family disappeared. They accepted my new culinary reality, and I traded my lunch hour for a time of prayer, meditation, and Bible Study.

Most importantly, the fast became an unanticipated time of growth for me. It seemed the longer I went without food, the more God poured His Spirit into me and I had a heightened awareness of His presence around me at all times. I also began to notice more of the things He cares about—namely, people. As a pastor, I worked with and served people as a part of my job, but until then I didn't really appreciate them. I interacted with them because God loved them, but not necessarily because I loved them. All of that changed during those forty days.

As I grew closer to God, my focus shifted toward loving His most cherished creations. The longer I went without eating, the more I saw God's hand feeding me with His strength and passion for others. I became less focused on the flavor of the food, and more focused on the aroma of God's love in the people around me.

When the time came to end the fast, I was reluctant. I knew my body needed the nourishment, but I feared losing the closeness and kinship with God. Now, almost five years later, the love for people that God grew in me continues to spill out through my work as a worship pastor and a Christian speaker and writer. I never dreamed that God would change me so drastically while I was praying for Him to use my church, but have come to this realization: For the church to be used in the mighty way we asked of Him, His Spirit must fill them to overflowing. That process begins with me...and with you.

Gary Chevalier is a worship pastor, speaker, and writer. He and his wife, Andrea, speak and teach on marriage/family and relationships via Internet broadcasts, retreats, conferences, and workshops. You can find out more about Gary and his ministry at www.garychevalier.com

Carole Klock

THINKING ABOUT THOUGHTS

LATELY, I'VE BEEN doing a lot of thinking about - thoughts. Do your thoughts ever come to you loudly? What I mean is, do they really bang around in your head, demanding they be thought right now? Thoughts show up in the most peculiar ways and sometimes at the most inconvenient times. Some are delightful and welcome, others not so much. We can be totally immersed in work or a project or a family situation and suddenly we're bombarded with unrelated thoughts that have no business being there.

Sometimes thoughts are like soft drops of dew. Do we ever see a dew drop appear? At what precise moment does that happen? We walk outside in the early morning and the grass glistens. There is our dew drop, one of millions of dew drops that make everything sparkle. Some thoughts are like that. They are the quiet, gentle thoughts that can bring a soft smile, a slight shrug of the shoulders and perhaps a fond memory or two to mull over and hold close for a moment.

There are times, however, when thoughts come upon me like cymbals crashing or dissonant horns blazing away. These are not peaceful, pleasant, dreamy thoughts. They are angry, bitter, sad and unwelcome taking me back over the years to times and places that I'd really rather forget. I remember times when my husband was serving with the Marines in a dangerous place and I was left alone to care for our three children. There were difficult times of wondering where the money to buy the food for next week's table would come from. The thoughts I least welcome take me back to a childhood painfully remembered; a time when insecurity was my constant companion. Days were long and filled with fear. Nights seemed endless and frightening. There was no Daddy there to read me a bedtime story. My mommy lived somewhere else and wasn't there to tuck me in each night. My foster parents simply sent me upstairs to bed. I was alone in a dark room convinced there were monsters under my bed or in my closet just waiting to jump out and grab me if I moved off my bed. I was often sleepless until the early morning hours. How I longed to grow up so that it would all be over.

Well, now I am grown up and it is all over. The security and peace I so longed for; all that was missing during those years are now part of my life. Everything is not perfect, of course, but I have joy and happiness. So why do these thoughts of bygone times come to me so rudely? Why do they intrude into the secure little world I've built for myself with all the force of a brass band on the 4th of July, or a jet plane roaring overhead, rattling windows and vibrating everything on the shelves? I don't want to think them, but they bounce around in my head, completely unbidden, competing with one another for my immediate attention. They demand time that I would not give them if I had a choice. I try hard to push them away into the dark corner of my mind I've reserved for them but they will not go. I want to close the door on them but they keep spilling out into the conscious portion of my mind. They may not all be unpleasant, but they are nagging and disturbing. The boundaries of the little territory of life I've mapped out for myself are no longer secure. I don't feel safe anymore. So why do they come? What possible reason could there be?

Deny these thoughts? I don't think so. I am convinced that these thoughts come to me as little gifts from my Heavenly Father. They remind me of where I've been and how far I've come with His help. His hand has been on my life from the beginning and as I look back, I see how He has worked in my life and changed things so completely. If I were to forget all these things I don't want to remember, then I'd also forget to thank my God for His goodness and for all the blessings He has heaped upon me. I have seen both sides of the coin: insecurity—security, unloved—loved, turmoil—peace. I can honestly say, fully aware of how much He loves me, "Thank you, Lord, for blessing me so much!"

Carole Klock was raised in foster care. She accepted Christ at the age of fifteen. Carole was co-editor of her high school newspaper and is a member of a writer's group in Colorado Springs, Colorado. Her passions are: family, writing, music, Miniature Schnauzers, and quilting.

Karen Hartung

DADDY'S LAP

AS I DRIFTED off to sleep, nagging thoughts of an unanswered e-mail lingered in my mind. Suddenly awakened by the irritating yelps of our little dog, my husband groaned as he dragged himself out of bed to find Ginger was simply demanding attention. As I lay there, I could not get that e-mail out of my mind, so I snuck into the computer room to see if it was there. My heart pounded as I saw it in my inbox. Could it be that things were getting better? Could it be a positive response? My hopes quickly faded as I read it.

As we snuggled back under our comfy duvet, I could not stop seeing the words on the computer screen. "No, we will not be coming—thanks anyway." A cold, impersonal, obligatory reply —not what you would expect from a close loved one. But because of our broken relationship, sadly, I was not surprised. The wounds of rejection opened once again. It hurt.

"I will keep in perfect peace—he whose mind is stayed on Thee—because he trusts in Thee." The verse I often recited when I was fighting sleep did not have its usual calming effect. Over and over I recited this in my mind, but sleep still would not come. I felt no type of peace, let alone perfect peace, I whined to God. I was trying to keep my mind on Him and trust Him to fix this broken relationship, but …

Tears started pouring down my cheeks. I wanted to scream and cry out loud, but I needed my husband to get back to sleep. If he knew I was upset, he would want to protect me and fix it for me, but this was not something he could fix. Quietly weeping, I thought of how broken relationships go against God's plan for us. The world started with the relationship of God the Father, the Son and the Holy Spirit. God sent His Son to earth to build that bridge for us to enter into relationship with Him. I was so thankful for the relationship I had with God, and was somewhat consoled knowing how He was also hurting because of this broken relationship and wanted to be included in it.

Thoughts of my childhood crept in. Dad was a wonderful man whom I loved dearly, but in his early years as a parent, he was not a good father. His addiction to alcohol and partying took precedence over being a dad. But once I had grown up and was able to forgive him, we established an amazing new father/daughter relationship. And then he died—far too soon. Oh, Dad, why did you have to die? I need you here now. I want to talk to you about this, sit on your lap, rest my head on your shoulder and cry. Cry and tell you all about my hurts so that you can make them all better.

And then it hit me. As a little girl, I had never experienced sitting on my daddy's lap. I lost it— the sobs came uncontrollably now. Thankfully, my husband was fast asleep. I remembered the times when my daughter had been scared and couldn't sleep. She loved when I consoled her with the words in Psalm 121, telling her God was sitting on a chair beside her bed, watching over her every breath, and keeping guard on her life all night long, never sleeping.

It was my turn now to be encouraged by these verses. "…he who watches over you will not slumber; indeed, he who watches over Israel will neither slumber nor sleep." Clutching my pillow, I closed my eyes and my sobbing stopped. And then, it was as if God was sitting by my bed. I sat up, slid across the sheets and onto His lap. Gently laying my head on His shoulder, through tears, I told Him all about my hurts. The peace I had been trying to find suddenly filled my soul. Out of this unexpected overflow, my Heavenly Father had momentarily become my earthly father. At long last, I was sitting on my "Daddy's" lap.

Karen Hartung has received a 'Certificate of Christian Studies' with honors at Canadian Southern Baptist Seminary, led Bible Study Fellowship and is presently involved in various ministries at Centre Street Church in Calgary, AB Canada. Karen and her husband, Garth live in Balzac, AB, Canada with their three children and can be contacted at hartung5@telus.net

Joneal Kirby

Legacy of the Heart

MY BIBLE READING this morning included Colossians 3:23, "Whatever you do, work at it with all your heart, as working for the Lord, not men." I've thought of this scripture countless times. The Father's Word encourages and informs my values and persistent approach to work and to ministry. But this output outlook also came from my father. On July 2 each year, I reminisce about my father's memorial service, where I, along with hundreds of family members and friends, jubilantly and sorrowfully celebrated his life and death. My father, my precious, funny Daddy, provided one of God's greatest gifts. He was committed as a parent with unconditional, guiding love. He lived a rich family life, a dedicated husband and father. Known by many, he worked to become a fond friend as he pursued people with a joyous intensity. He had a warm way of talking with someone that made them feel as if they were the most special person he had ever known. His faith in God was deep and rich. My dad was completely in love with the Lord's church, where he served with his whole heart as a teacher, a deacon, and an elder.

All who knew him would confirm that my dad loved to work. He greeted every day as an adventure, as if he'd never been to the office before. He also taught us that nothing was a big deal that could not be prayed about or worked through with the right faith and attitude. Dad's Marine Corps training shared in shaping his values about work. As a young sergeant, his developing work ethic moved smoothly into his transition to civilian life where he took on the task of completing an engineering degree by attending fulltime day classes. In order to support his wife and five children, he did what he had to do, and worked night jobs.

Dad's work ethic was: work hard at whatever is necessary, enthusiastically as if working for the Lord. A story from his childhood illustrates this fearless attitude. As he was entering high school, his older brother had just graduated and enlisted in the Navy. Before leaving for his training, his brother asked Dad if he wanted his job at the school, sweeping up the classrooms each morning and cleaning out the trash. This janitor job had been his brother's for several years and he knew it was just a matter of asking the school principal about it, to get the job for my dad. The job only paid a dollar a day and in addition to cleaning the school, he also was responsible for opening the school each morning. As a fourteen-year-old kid, walking alone into that huge, old school early in the morning was terrifying. He often walked in on some rough drifter who had camped out in the school sick room. His biggest fright though came from the total darkness of the school's halls. Describing it as the deepest darkness, when he told the story, Dad held his hand in front of his face and said in the pitch black he could not even see it. He was also startled by his own jarring footsteps as he walked the weathered hardwood floors. He confessed how distressing those lonely, dark, quiet mornings were. Until, he said, he could reach for and find the light switches. He opened the school door and groped along the wall for the row of switches, and he turned on the panels of four and five switches all at the same time. Then the lights brilliantly glared bright as day in the hallways. Dad said he could then walk down the hall turning on every light in every room as he did. And finally, "I felt safe enough so I could get to work."

In remembering it is a comfort to believe when Daddy was approaching his death, Jesus went ahead of him down the hall and turned on the lights in Heaven. I know my Daddy was safe. And Dad knew he was safe. And knowing my Dad -- when he got there, he went right to work.

My dad's willingness to work at whatever it took to produce a friend, protect his country, or provide for his family blended seamlessly with a joyful enthusiasm for life. He showed me and taught me the grace of work that comes out of an overflowing heart.

Joneal Kirby, Ph.D., is a unique combination of marriage therapist, radio and television speaker, women's ministry leader, and parenting educator. Her unique speaking and writing style combines practical advice, biblical insights, and humor rooted in her passion for strengthening families.

Marilyn Neuber-Larson

FAITHFUL FURRY FRIEND

AFTER TWENTY-FIVE YEARS, I struggled with the intense reality of being alone and single again.

Sam, my hundred-pound Alaskan malamute, shared my grief. As friend and protector, he always helped me answer the doorbell. The caller invariably backed up two steps, when greeted by such a huge, wolf-like dog.

One evening, Sam nudged me with his wet nose when I dressed to go out with some women from church. I knew he wished I'd stay with him. By the middle of the evening I too, wished I'd stayed home. At midnight we friends stood and shrugged into our coats. I'd been ready to slip away much earlier.

The night air sent an icy chill down my back when they dropped me at my car and drove away. I danced on the accelerator, but my starter growled and didn't want to catch. Who in the world could I ask for help at this hour?

Alone in the pitch-blackness I shivered, easing my foot off the gas, and waited while my heart pounded as if it would jump through my chest. Again and again I turned the key. Finally the engine sputtered, and grudgingly chugged and groaned up the hill. My teeth chattered in terror as my foot jerked against the pedal all the way home.

In the kitchen, Sam's huge tail beat a tattoo against the door. I knelt and hugged his neck, buried my face in his warm fur, and shared his relief.

"I'm really glad to be back home with you, Sammy Shoe. Are you ready for your cookie?" I stood and gave him his nightly dog biscuit.

The house was chilly as I headed to bed. Shivering, I piled two extra blankets on top of the bedspread, but sleep was evasive and I couldn't get warm.

"Oh God," I prayed, "I'm so scared and alone. Help me trust you, Jesus."

I drifted into a semi-conscious stupor, but in the middle of the night, I awakened weeping. Sadness erupted, and my bellowing sobs escalated into mournful wails. Finally, I sat up to catch my breath—and cry.

Dog tags jingled as Sam bounded down the hall. At the doorway, he took his usual gigantic leap, and landed on the bed. A full moon shone from behind clouds, splashing silver light across the room.

Sam stared at me blubbering. He leaned so close his slanted-eyes crossed. Then he tilted his head until his nose pointed to the ceiling. His white chin whiskers quivered in the moonlight. "Woo-woo-w-o-o-o," he bayed. "Woo-woo-w-o-o-o.

I threw my arms around his furry neck, and we howled together in a loud lament, sharing our grief. After a while, with my arms still wrapped around Sam's neck, we collapsed and drifted off to sleep.

The next morning, bright sunlight shimmered, and I woke with a peace I hadn't felt before. A hint of spring hung in the air.

"Thanks, Lord, for sending Sam to mourn with me last night. I know he's hurting too."

I opened the door and my huge dog trotted outside. When the coffee was ready, I reached for my Bible and devotional booklet, and turned to the first chapter of Joshua. The words seemed to jump off the page: "Be strong and courageous. Do not be terrified; do not be discouraged, for the Lord your God will be with you wherever you go" (Joshua 1:9 NIV).

The phone rang. My friend, Elsie, always sensed when I needed encouragement. "Hi, I'm on my way out and don't have time to talk. I just want to tell you something. Every step you take, you won't have to take again. Bye."

I scribbled that awesome verse and Elsie's encouraging words on a scrap of paper and stuck it on the refrigerator. It stayed there for a year.

It reminds me, I'm never alone because my awesome Lord is always with me, and even when life turned cold and dark, God sent me a faithful, furry friend.

Marilyn Neuber-Larson is an author and speaker who lives in Albuquerque, New Mexico. After ten years of being single, she married her pumpkin-farmer husband, Bill, and became the Pumpkin Queen. She continues to be awestruck at God's answers to prayer.

Lawrence J. Clark

JESUS FREAKS

WHAT IS UP with these Jesus Freaks?" I muttered aloud as I drove away from the run-down duplex, chiding myself for wasting time doing a demonstration for people who obviously couldn't afford to make a purchase. It was my third month as a Rainbow sales representative, and I should have known better. The $495 price tag of the water filtration home cleaning units (known to some as vacuum cleaners) was more than most people in the farming and factory towns of Southern Maine could afford. Due to some creative financing and a well-rehearsed demonstration, though, I had done fairly well so far. I was the region's top salesman the previous month and was well on my way to a repeat performance.

This last couple, though, seemed more intent on preaching to me than purchasing one of our fine machines. I had just turned eighteen, and they were not much older than me. The husband had the classic geek look, with a crew cut, black plastic glasses, and a short-sleeved white shirt. His wife had, well, no style at all, and seemed to be straight off the farm.

"Did you know," Mr. Geek began as I was setting up for my demo, "if you drink a beer, it's like lighting a firecracker and dropping it down into your stomach?"

"Is that so?" I said, trying hard to be polite. I was not much of a drinker, but I knew enough to realize this guy was just a few steps off the turnip truck.

"And if you smoke a cigarette, your lungs could explode," Mrs. Geek chimed in.

"Interesting," I said.

"We're Christians, so of course we don't do any of those things," said Mr. Geek. "You should be a Christian, too."

I can't remember my response, but I remember thinking I didn't want to be anything like these people or have anything to do with their brand of religion. Sure, I believed in God, but only in a vague sense. I remember getting into an argument with my atheist friend, George; I told him he was an idiot for not believing in God, for which I received a black eye. That was about the closest thing I had ever done to sharing my faith, such as it was, with another human being.

I had a 1972 Mercury Capri and a cute girlfriend and was making $400 a week without a high school diploma. What did I have in common with a couple of straight-laced nerds who believed such things and couldn't even afford a decent vacuum cleaner? Wasn't life all about making money and having fun? They certainly didn't seem like they were having much fun.

What I didn't know, though, was that God has the best sense of humor of all of us; in fact, from what I've learned since, he invented the whole concept.

The very next night, I was at another couple's house and noticed an enormous white Bible on the table.

"Oh, no," I thought, "here we go again."

"Nice Bible," I said. Always compliment something in the house, my sales manager had taught me. Anyway, this couple seemed a little more normal.

"Sure is," said Mr. More Normal Guy. "Ever read it?"

"Uh, sure," I said, laying out the eleven attachments on the floor.

"No, I mean, have you ever really read it?"

"Not lately . . ." I said.

"Mind if I show you something?"

"Sure."

He opened the gigantic book as Mrs. More Normal Guy smiled sweetly and handed me a cup of tea.

"For God so loved the world that He gave his only begotten Son. Do you believe that?"

"Well, yeah, that's Jesus."

He then read some other verses, explaining that I needed to accept these things in order to be saved from my sins; it all sounded perfectly logical and reasonable to me. The next thing I knew, I was kneeling on the floor, vacuum hose in one hand, praying for Jesus to come into my heart.

For some reason, God had used the couple from the previous night to prepare me for this special moment. Mr. More Normal Guy didn't buy a vacuum either, but for some reason I didn't care. He had sold me something worth much more than a hundred dollar commission. I laughed aloud as I slowly drove the back way home, basking in the moment with God's love now flowing around and through His newest "Jesus Freak."

Lawrence J. Clark is an author, speaker, and songwriter who frequently speaks and performs in schools, churches, and libraries. He is co-founder, with his wife Kristen, of HisWitness.org and NewBeginningsMarriage.org, for which he writes a regular column based on personality theory, marriage, and men's issues.

Debbie Hannah Skinner

SNIPPING THE APRON STRINGS

SHE LOOKED AT me and cried. Sniffle.

I looked at her and did the same. Double sniffle.

Weepy. That's the best word to describe the days and weeks leading up to when our only child left for college.

Throughout the summer months between her high school graduation and freshman orientation, frequent hugs, handholds, and kisses on the cheek became the norm. I don't think she was convinced she was ready to pack up her belongings and move to a college located four and a half hours away from home. I certainly wasn't.

As a mom, I was terrified. Had I prepared her for what she would encounter in college? Would she survive her freshman year?

It took a peculiar, perfectly timed "scissor cut" from God, delivered precisely on the day before she started college, to calm my fears.

Dorm check-in was at 10 a.m. on a Saturday and the only way we could be there on time was to leave a day early and spend the night in a hotel near the university. I don't know if it was the stress of sorting, packing, and moving her most valued possessions or the vague uncertainties surrounding her future in a strange new place, but my precious girl was like a different person from the moment we left our driveway. She was "in a mood," as my grandmother would say. It was a very dark one indeed.

The weather outside was bright and sunny, but as I sat beside her in the passenger seat while she drove, the atmosphere inside the car was far from lovey-dovey-sniffly-weepy. It was the opposite: overcast, stormy, and down right ornery. For some reason, she was upset and her anger was aimed firmly in one direction— at me.

Gone were the days of sweetness and light. Every topic of conversation we began ended with a snippy comment or sharp answer, which was so out of character for her. Like oil and water, we seemed to disagreed on everything that day, from where to stop for lunch, to the radio volume, to who would be the next relief driver for her dad (who was sheltered from the storm in the car ahead of us).

I wanted to drive his car because it gave me a chance for peace, quiet, and calm. She wanted to drive his car to get away from me. I'll never forget looking at my watch at two o'clock that Friday afternoon and thinking to myself, "I wonder if the college would mind if we just drop her off a day early..."

That's when I started laughing.

What a turn around our mother-daughter team was experiencing! In a matter of hours, we had shifted from grieving over letting one another go to chomping at the bit to get away from each other. The irony of the scene that day juxtaposed against our tearful summer flooded my heart with reassurance from the Lord that all would be well.

Even though neither of us could articulate our feelings at the time, what happened between us was simple. She was ready to go. I was ready for her to go. It was time for the apron strings to be cut.

As I look back at that day, I'm reminded of how gracious the Lord was to give us a sweet, sniffling summer together, a time of leisurely lunches and long talks. We even had a special "girl trip" together in June that affirmed our love and care for one another. I had watched friends whose kids were ready to leave for college long before their senior year in high school even began. Their families subsequently spent a year in turmoil as teenagers, longing to leave home, spread their wings of independence and knocked people over in the process.

Our family never experienced that. But on the very day when we needed it, within hours of the time we had to drop her off at college, it was as though the Lord gently took out a big pair of scissors and — snip, snip, snip — the apron strings were gently cut so we could both let go and move on. His timing could not have been more perfect.

We both needed reassurance that it was time for her to move on. It came flowing down packaged in a peculiar day full of snippy conversations and frazzled feelings.

That was exactly what we both needed.

Debbie Hannah Skinner is a speaker/artist/writer known as "The Bible Teacher with a Paintbrush." Formerly a public school teacher, she now weaves her words and watercolors with wisdom from Scripture as she speaks to women's groups around the United States. Debbie's art appears on the cover of *Out of the Overflow.* You can learn more about her work at www.dhskinner.com.

Joe Bowden

GOD OF THE PUTTY KNIFE

I REMEMBER THE exact date when it all fell apart and I broke down. Most of us guy types tend to hide facts that show our humanity and many just don't talk about them period. Maybe it is the testosterone gene or just human pride when we know we have reached the end of our ropes and the future seems to be out of options.

It all started long before that fitful day. I had left the university system with plans to start a new business near our parents in hope that our children would have the honor of knowing their grandparents on a daily basis. However the move back was just another notch in the ratchet of tension building around my family.

The extended family dynamics we experienced as children and teens had changed significantly in the fifteen-year absence, for college and jobs distant from home.

Arrival back home started a slide into more and more responsibilities for my wife now with two preschool children and a husband who was gone too much in an attempt to grow our business into the black.

Let me pause here and offer an example of the lose-lose situations surrounding my wife at this time. When she was with her grandmother she had to side with her quirks and when she was with her aunt she had to side with her quirks. This was not too bad until an upcoming family event where both her aunt and grandmother were in attendance. The stress of having to choose one over the other along with the usual banter about how we should raise our children became the proverbial straw and with the help of our family doctor she was admitted to the hospital and thus avoiding the mine field of choosing one over the other.

With my wife in the hospital with a nervous breakdown and our children staying at their uncle's house I found my self totally alone in my living room with the prospect it may be this way for a time.

TV 's distractions only lasted a few hours and as I grew more and more melancholy my emotions began to break through the male mystic and my head was about to explode. Tears flooded down my cheeks and I fell to the floor in front of the living room sofa. Soon the tears began to dry and a feeling of helplessness bloomed and took over my thoughts. *What can I do? How can I work and take care of my children at the same time? How will my wife take the stress of healing?* These and many other grey thoughts flooded my mind until in desperation I began to pray.

All I remember of that prayer was "God, I don't know what to do. Please help me." I can't explain what happened next but a sense of calm filled the room until all I could think of was *It can't be this easy;* God does not work this way. God parts the Red Sea and things like that, not bringing calm to a stormy life. Then bits scripture in a whirl invaded my consciousness "My yolk is easy," "Come follow Me," "Don't worry about the troubles of today"...

It has been nearly thirty years since that fitful day when I came to grips with just who God really is. The road has had bumps and ruts to contend with, but I know now that He is a friend, a Father and a faithful provider.

I have used this hard-learned principle in many Sunday School applications. I call it the "Splat Effect." This is when God lets us go faster and faster until .. Splat, we hit the wall, then, God through the Holy Spirit scrapes us off the wall with a putty knife. Then in careful love reforms, remolds, and reshapes us unto vessels fit for His service.

Dr. Joe Bowden, Ph.D. is first and foremost a teacher who enjoys story. He is a husband, environmental biochemist, father, and grandfather. Joe lives in Durango, CO with his wife Elaine where they both write for enjoyment, edification, and encouragement.

Connie Leonard

SONSHINE IN MY SOUL

> "Peace I leave with you; my peace I give you. I do not give to you as the world gives. Do not let your hearts be troubled and do not be afraid."
>
> —John 14:27 NIV

I LEFT IN plenty of time to make the hour-long drive to get my grandchildren from the temporary babysitter, but an accident on the highway brought traffic to a standstill. Listening to inspirational music didn't stop the gray clouds from permeating my mood.

Finally the highway cleared, and movement resumed. As I turned onto a long stretch of two-lane highway, the heavens exploded with a torrential downpour. The ominous clouds completely obscured the sunlight. Blinded by the rain and the lights of oncoming cars, anxiety built. I began to pray, *Dear Lord, please don't let me have an accident. I have to get to my grandchildren.*

When the two-lane road turned into a four-lane highway, the rain let up, and I could see once again. I relaxed and began to pray about my son's failed marriage and my precious grandchildren. "I Can Only Imagine" rang from my cell phone. Seeing my brother's name at 7:30 in the morning didn't require much imagination to realize something was wrong.

"Sis, I'm on my way to the hospital. They think Mom had a stroke. I'll call you as soon as I find out what's going on."

I blinked back tears. "Okay." *Lord, please let my mother be okay. What would we do without her?*

The old hymn "Whispering Hope" began playing on the CD player:

"Soft as the voice of an angel,
Breathing a lesson unheard,
Hope with a gentle persuasion
Whispers her comforting word:
Wait til the darkness is over,
Wait till the tempest is done
Hope for the sunshine tomorrow,
After the shower is gone."

Suddenly beams of light burst through the darkness, piercing my eyes. Squinting, I looked in amazement at the sight before me: Sunlight formed a perfect star, dispelling the gloom, bringing hope and peace to my soul.

The voice of God whispered in my heart. "I am the light of the world. In me there is no darkness." The tension eased away.

Lord, why do I worry when I have prayer at my disposal? You have promised to give us peace in all situations when we give our cares and concerns to you. Thank you for your deliverance in the past, for all you are doing now whether we see it or not, and for the good you are planning to do in the future.

The beautiful picture of the star of light shining through darkness will remain with me forever. All is good. My mother recovered, I continue to pray for my son's family as I praise God for every opportunity to be with my grandchildren. Storms will come again, but they will always be followed by Sonshine.

Connie Lewis Leonard lives in Texas with her husband of over forty years. They have two grown children, two grandchildren, and three dogs. Her hobbies include reading, baking, gardening, and scrapbooking. Since retiring from teaching, she plans to follow a life-long dream and passion for writing.

Dalton Jantzen

Learning to Argue with God and Win!

WHEN WAS THE last time you argued with God? Argued. You know, that's when He says something and you disagree. In the past I knew the difference between arguing with my wife and arguing with God in that He didn't go past the first two go-rounds. God doesn't repeat Himself He just lets me talk until I run out of words. It's the deafening silence that tells me the argument is over.

"Dalton, do this."

"Lord, why would I do that? I don't think so. What do you mean?"

Silence.

"Now wait a minute Lord, come back here. You were talking to me. You know I don't want to have to do that. Lord? Are You there? Lord...."

Silence.

Oh, how I would love to think that He wins when that happens, but just giving in is no win for either of us. Giving in is not the same as Him winning because we will revisit the issue until I let Him win rightfully. Of course He wins, He's God. But, if I choose to yield first instead of going on and on incessantly, then it can be a win for both of us. My surrender pleases Him and me.

My big argument with God started late last year. For seven years I labored with God to birth and grow a ministry He inspired and loved. Then reaching what looked to many like the beginning of a whole new exciting level of growth, we peaked. Just two months after He provided the cash to purchase the 20 acres He promised; the bottom began to drop out. It was barely noticeable at first, but then it just started falling away.

We ran the numbers and realized that we couldn't sustain the budget. My doubts ended when we had to lay off our staff; and then our volunteers and even some key team members stopped calling. They were facing personal challenges that caused them to have to pull back on their investment of time and energy in the ministry. They didn't want to but their choice was simple; it was either this or that, but not both this and that. And our ministry was that.

By Easter morning I could no longer avoid the conversation with God. On Easter Sundays my wife and I attend two or three worship services with church families we have worked closely with during the year. We were at the last service late that morning and I silently stood with my eyes closed, lost in the praise and worship, when God spoke.

"Dalton, let it go. I don't want you to worry about this anymore. You don't have to be responsible for the retreat center any more. It's not your problem. I got it."

"But Lord! We have prayed for your Spirit to walk freely around the place. You remember the people who tell how they sense Your Presence - just driving on the property? What will happen if..."

This time He didn't let me finish; He interrupted me, "Dalton. It's just dirt and stucco!"

Silence...

And I was the one who was silent.

He had the last word. I was through arguing.

Then I began to sense weight falling off of my shoulders. I looked around and there was nothing on the floor behind me, but I felt lighter. The praise time was over and I was sitting in my chair listening to the message but there was music going on inside of me; gentle praise and joy. I began to sense peace, the kind of peace I had not experienced in months.

The point of surrender is the beginning of peace. You don't have to argue to get to surrender, but God is willing to argue if necessary to get you there. To Him it's worth the argument if you end up with peace.

Seven months later the music still plays inside me. The Lord has provided a couple who want to buy the property to establish and operate a prayer retreat center in our region. They found our property to be perfect for fulfilling the God-dream they've had for twenty years.

You can't win with Him if you stay in the conversation. I recommend you surrender early, and "...be still and KNOW that I am God."

Dalton Jantzen and his wife Vicki minister side by side through 30 60 100 Ministries, Inc. providing coaching and equipping tools for servant leaders across North and South America, Europe and SE Asia. Their focus is to equip believers to challenge their culture until common Christian complacency becomes the abnormality.

Lessie Harvey

God's Overflow

WHERE IN MY life could I truly say that I have witnessed or experienced God's overflow? Naturally my first thoughts centered on my material possessions. Even though I considered myself comfortable, neither my family nor friends would say I had great wealth, possessions, or many of the material comforts others desired. If I had to measure my life by the standards of those who seek wealth, possessions, or the latest material comforts, I guess I would be far from the front of the line.

So as of November 10, 2010, God's overflow has not been financial or material outpourings in my life.

Overflow. Where in my life do I have more than enough so that I can freely share with others and still have more than enough for myself? I then thought of my relationships. Some of my personal relationships are exceptional. I truly enjoy the company of certain people because we encourage, support, and help each other become a better person. But, and there's always that pesky but, there are some relationships in my life that desperately need intervention. At this point, I'm ready for counseling or a miracle from God these bad relationships are in need of resuscitation and reconciliation. Resuscitation to bring them back to life and reconciliation to bring them back into balance.

Unfortunately, I would have to say that as of November 10, 2010, God's overflow has not been in the personal relationships in my life.

Most people seek financial or material blessings as a confirmation of personal success. If I depended on those, I would consider myself a failure, but I'm not a failure. Others seek power in relationships. I freely admit I need counseling or a miracle from God, so I guess my success does not stem from my personal relationships.

I finally had to ask myself why I consider myself successful when nothing around me shows that I am successful according to the standards of others. That's when I realized God's abundance and overflow in my life. It was not outside but within me!

For more than thirty years God has been working in me. The arrogant, self-sufficient, me-centered person is no longer the dominant ruler of my life. Through God's love, patience, faithfulness, mercy, and grace I am transforming into a new creation. I know this sounds mushy and no one likes mushy, but it is the path to God's overflow for me

For most of my life, I never felt truly loved by anyone. As long as I did what others wanted me to do, yes I felt loved. It was when I didn't respond or act the way others wanted me to that I didn't feel loved by them. I could not understand why their love depended on my actions. What if I thought or acted differently from them? To me, it didn't mean that I loved them less. Why should they love me less because of my actions or feelings?

Regardless of what I thought or how I acted, I never felt that God withheld His love from me. It seemed as though He always sent someone to show me the way I should go or how I should act. He taught me through His Word. It seemed that whenever I was struggling with how I should think or behave in certain situations, the Bible passage I happened to read was exactly what I needed to shape my thinking or behavior. Condemnation was never part of the learning process.

That's how I learned God's patience and faithfulness. His patience because I'm still learning how to apply a principle or precept I learned more than thirty years ago. His faithfulness because He continues to walk with and encourage me when I stumble or fall after all these years. It seems as though He refuses to give up on me. Now that's love exemplified and multiplied.

Another way of describing the awesome love of God is His grace and mercy to me. Even when I don't deserve God's love, He gives it to me. Whenever I acknowledge my disobedience and rebellion against God's Word, it's as though He rejoices and pours out His goodness in my life. I experience the same forgiveness, acceptance, and joy the prodigal son must have felt when his father forgave and honored him.

From the overflow of God's goodness in my life, I choose to serve Him through speaking, writing, or serving others so that they may get a glimpse or experience a fragment of God's goodness to me.

I enjoy exercising the gift of hospitality because it gives me the opportunity to share the overflow of God's love, patience, faithfulness, mercy, and grace to all those in my circle of influence.

Lessie Harvey is a CLASS faculty member, writer, and speaker living in Maryland. Lessie is the author of *Becoming God's Vessel of Honor.* Her desire is to encourage, empower, and equip to fulfill their calling.

Kathi Lipp

WHATEVER

I AM DEFINITELY not a perfectionist in most areas of my life - one look at my garage and you will see I can be downright casual in my approach to organizing - but I get so frustrated with myself in those areas that a perfectionistic spirit rears its ugly head in my life.

It can happen when we have people coming over to the house (especially people I don't know very well). I have a list and I'm not afraid to unleash it on those around me. My kids duck for cover and the dog hides under the bed. There was a time in our marriage when my husband, Roger, thought it would be easier just not to have friends than to go through the Extreme Home Makeover before new visitors came around.

I know that this perfectionism streak comes directly from my need to please, and my need to please comes from fear.

- Fear that someone is going to think less of me
- Fear that someone is going to find out "the truth" about me
- Fear that I'm going to let someone down

When I'm letting fear rule my life is when I stop letting God do that job. I wrestle back and forth for control. All because I'm afraid to let go and say, "OK God, Whatever."

When I'm walking with Christ, daily committing myself to Him, I am not walking in fear. I'm not afraid of the consequences of life (OK, less afraid of the consequences) because I understand on every level I am not the one in control of where I end up.

1 John 4:18 says: "There is no fear in love. But perfect love drives out fear, because fear has to do with punishment. The one who fears is not made perfect in love."

Walking in Christ's love is freedom.

- Freedom from the need to control.
- Freedom from fear.
- Freedom from the need to come off as perfect.

When I approach God with my hands open and say, "OK God. Whatever…." that is when I experience the freedom that only comes from trusting Him completely.

So the next time you come on over to my house, if you see Jake the puggle out from under the bed, and my kids walking freely about, you can be assured that I have taken some small steps towards trusting God for the Whatever He has in store for me.

Kathi Lipp is a speaker and the author of *The Husband Project* and *The Marriage Project*, both with Harvest House Publishers. Her website is www.kathilipp.com

Robin Cowin

Infinite Overflow

OUR GUEST WAS a man spouting all kinds of things that were on the edge of truth but not quite there. We engaged him in order to keep him from leading other customers in our coffee house astray. He soon caught on to what we were doing and became agitated. The shadow of understanding that crossed his face was quickly followed by a cloud of anger.

"Go to hell," the unwelcome visitor exclaimed.

"Out of the abundance of the mouth, the heart speaks," my friend muttered loud enough for us to hear. We began to laugh and our venting visitor departed quickly. We were all laughing because we knew the verse had been deliberately misquoted but in a way that seemed appropriate at the time. Jesus said, "Out of the abundance of the *heart* the *mouth* speaks."

Misquoting the verse doesn't change the meaning. Rather, it serves as an introduction to commentary on its meaning. When we are wrapped up in ourselves and the sound of our own voices we cannot hear anyone else, including God. Jesus was saying the heart contains whatever we allow in and when the heart overflows it does so through the mouth. If we are full of ourselves or things of the world that is what comes out of us when we talk. If we are full of God then God will flow out in our conversation.

That is where Jesus was going when he was asked by a lawyer about the greatest commandment. He pointed back to the law which says the first command is to love God with all our hearts, minds, soul, and strength. Then he went a step further with the second most important commandment, to love your neighbor as yourself. His disciple, John, would later write to the church, "If anyone says, 'I love God,' yet hates his brother, he is a liar…the one who loves God must also love his brother." The overflow of loving God is to love your neighbor; the overflow of loving your neighbor is fulfilling the great commission to go into all the world with the Gospel.

Paul joins the conversation in his advice to his young protégé, Timothy. He tells Timothy there is a goal to all that he is teaching him. That goal is love from a pure heart, a good conscience, and a sincere faith.

The overflow of God's love is the great commandment. Our love for him comes from a pure heart. This is not something we do ourselves. Rather it is something God does for us when by his mercy he gives us grace. A pure heart comes from loving God with all your heart, soul, mind, and strength. That kind of love cannot be bottled up. Love from a heart made pure by grace overflows in our conversation and our actions.

The overflow of God's love is a good conscience. We need to reach our neighbor across the street. A good conscience comes from loving your neighbor as yourself. You cannot truly love your neighbor unless you love God too. Loving God overflows into loving your neighbor. You also cannot truly love God unless you love your neighbor too.

The overflow of God's love is the Great Commission to reach around the world. A sincere faith is an open letter. Sincere means, "without wax," and was originally added to love letters to show that one's love was for all to see. We are all called to go around the world with the gospel no matter where your world is. A sincere faith is an open invitation to his grace.

Our visitor in the coffee house expressed his true heart. He loved neither us nor God and his heart was void of God's grace. We learned a lesson that day as well. Our laughter had driven him away even though we were laughing at the misquote and not him.

Out of the overflow the mouth says what the heart contains. A heart full of his grace cannot be kept to ourselves.

Robin H. Cowin has been a Baptist pastor in Oklahoma and Arkansas for over thirty years. He and his wife Joyce have four children and five grandchildren. He has written studies to prepare mission teams and encourage couples and men's ministries. He writes sermons, a blog, and has written Bible lessons for the Arkansas Baptist News.

Judy Parker

ADOPTION AT A COST

"ARE YOU NUTS?" My husband laughed as I made the suggestion to him.

"Yes, but I still think it's time Nicholas had a dog. Every little boy needs a dog and he wants one so much."

Rolling his eyes, my husband smiled. "Okay."

We had to choose carefully though. Living in a household with four children, a cat, a hamster, two parakeets, and a fish, the dog needed to coexist with others and not eat the smaller members of the family.

After praying for just the right dog, my husband and I ventured into the local animal shelter. We discovered a calm, golden Labrador Retriever. Housebroken already, he wasn't spastic like the other creatures begging for a home. His pleading eyes drew me in and I melted instantly.

Filled with excitement we brought him home and led him into the backyard. Chaos erupted. Kids screamed with surprise and delight while the dog raced around in a frenzy. He plunged into our small water fountain, broke the nozzle and spewed water everywhere. Frantically, he made a beeline for my precious vegetable garden.

"No, no, no!" I screamed trying to tackle him before he trampled my ripening Beefstake tomatoes.

We finally cornered the dog and calmed him down a bit. After a few minutes of petting and discussion, we let Kenai, our newly christened family member, into the house.

He celebrated by peeing on the carpet.

"I thought he was house broken?" my husband hollered while trying to get Kenai back outside.

"That's what they said at the shelter," I mumbled looking for the carpet cleaner. "Good grief. What's up with this dog?"

"No wonder he was at the shelter," my husband said.

Doubts began to fill my mind as I scrubbed the carpet. But, we had prayed about this dog. We thought he was the right one. Had we heard God wrong?

Those doubts increased when we discovered Kenai was sick. He didn't have a laid back personality, but Kennel Cough which turned into pneumonia. Numerous trips to the vet, IV's, and antibiotics amounted to more money than we could imagine. This was not what we had envisioned when we brought Kenai home.

Lying on the floor with his head on my lap, Kenai struggled for air as I prayed for answers. I stroked his silky ears and rubbed his chest. Somehow, he had managed to win my heart despite his bad behavior and illness.

More trouble ensued as Kenai regained his appetite, especially for socks, shoes, rugs, furniture, and walls.

And he constantly scratched himself and licked his feet.

"This dog does not have fleas!" I screamed in exasperation one day. "Why is he so itchy? Why does he want to chew his feet off?" Looking carefully at the raw spot on his foot, I knew another trip to the vet must follow.

Sighing, I shook my head. "Lord, what have I done? Grass! How can a dog be allergic to grass? He's a dog! I am NOT going to spend $200 every six months for allergy shots. I don't care how bad he itches."

I locked myself in the bathroom, hoping to be left alone for a few minutes. How could God let us pick out such a loser dog? How could we afford to keep him? But how could we give him back? Every one of us loved him and we were committed.

Kenai rattled the door as he tried to get in. Reluctantly I opened it. He rushed inside and buried his cold nose in my neck and licked my face.

All at once I was overcome with the thought I was just like Kenai, full of problems, sickness, and annoying habits. I unintentionally destroyed things. I sinned frequently and even my righteous acts could never be good enough. My adoption came with a price, God's only Son. He adopted me anyway because of His love and commitment to me.

Tears filled my eyes as I hugged Kenai tightly. "Lord, thank you for reminding me just how much you love me and that you always will despite my bad habits."

Choosing Kenai had not been a mistake. God just wanted to remind me of His limitless love for me.

Judy Parker juggles freelance writing, homeschooling, and chauffeuring kids from one activity to the next. After 20 years of following her husband around the world with the Air Force, she has finally settled down in Anchorage, AK. She enjoys hiking, fishing and cross-country skiing with her husband and four children.

Ruth Marquez West

Vanity Pressed

"A good man out of the good treasure of his heart brings forth that which is good; and an evil man out of the evil treasure of his heart brings forth that which is evil; for of the abundance of the heart his mouth speaks."

—Luke 6:45

WHY? IS THE expression on my daughter's face as I remove items from the bags she has proudly filled during weekend cleanup of Mom's house. Determined, I continue sorting through perfectly good items, intent on attributing worth to what has long since diminished in value for good reason. Next on my list is inspecting my son's yard work.

Quietly enduring scrutiny of his weed bucket, he bites his lip after being dispatched to work on both sides of the house for more evidence of his efforts. Dejected but obedient, he returns to work in the hot sun.

No doubt my family wishes, on occasion, that Mom had a built-in grace checker. Confessing my shortfall, I realize that, in fact, I possess a grace checker. It is in my heart cleansed with God's mercy. Grappling with the Truth that what I speak and write flows from deep within me, I am troubled that perhaps I aspire to inspire but am more prone to express with excess, liberally editing the intentions of others.

Yet God's standard for His work in my life and writing is not just word count, syntax, or proper presentation for all occasions. His ideal is not whether my words win the approval of others. Caring nothing about what fills volumes to overflowing, He cares, rather, that the fullness of Christ in my heart is the source of the overflow.

At this thought, I shrink away, pondering what a journey to the core of me will expose. In prayer and reflection, I am face-to-face with fear about what God finds in the crowded room of my heart where He lives. A faint fragrance of hope lingers amid the dark memories and leftover discontent in this chamber. Records of wrongs and once-shiny trophies are hidden under scribbled pages and plans that are strewn everywhere. It is now my turn to tidy up, and I rush around, desperately filling bags to the brim. But before long, I am overwhelmed by the task.

Finally, I collapse into a stained little chair with barely room for sobbing. I cannot look up, knowing that my Father is here. The realization that He, alone, is the lifter of my head fills the moment. In complete stillness, I ponder the vanity of my words over a lifetime. I wonder how many thousands of times I have missed the occasion of blessing others, offering only instruction and evaluation instead. Battling an onslaught of condemning thoughts, I renounce ever writing again apart from God's leading, as volumes stare back at me from dusty shelves.

My thoughts gradually shift to the awareness of God's sorting through the bags and pages I have filled. He seems to be rummaging through the mire of my abandoned trinkets and words. Removing nothing, He conveys a distinct disinterest in my assistance with His finishing work here. The echo of my doubt begins to subside.

"I am here for my treasure, little one," my heart hears in the soft light. "I am here for you."

Ruth Marquez West writes and co-edits a k-12 online education news publication in Denver, Colorado. Her work in training and instructional design, marketing, communications and public relations, as well as numerous articles on the reality of at-risk youth, have all influenced her writing and editorial perspective.

Terry Burns

HEART PRAYER

HAVE YOU EVER prayed a heart prayer? Perhaps like me you have and just didn't have a name for it. That would make sense to not have anything to call it since it's a prayer that has no words in it.

It happens when life puts us on our knees and we are so devastated, or so sad, or so grief stricken that our heads don't work. We're fuzzy and disoriented and our every sensation is wrapped in pain. Our chests are tight and there's a lump in our throats and there are no words to say what we are feeling because our brains won't or can't put the words together.

Suddenly we are aware that something is going up anyway, that our heart is talking directly to God, and since the words aren't there we don't know what's being said, but we know pure thoughts and feelings are being directly transmitted.

And we're just as sure that it's being heard.

It can be just the opposite as well. We can be so happy, so overcome with joy that there are no words big enough and grand enough to say what is in our hearts. As a writer, words are my business and it's hard to admit that sometimes mere words are just not enough. Some feelings can't be contained in ink and paper, like the first time I looked on a child or grandchild that was my very own or when I looked across at my wife during the marriage ceremony. The feelings were there, and they were mammoth and powerful, overflowing my heart and mind, and were too much to be contained by either so they just poured out on their own and went directly to God. No words, just pure, concentrated love and praise.

Have you ever prayed a heart prayer? I hope so. I hope there have been a lot of them, because whether it comes from a base of utter despair or intense joy, it's the closest we will ever get to God until the day we go to meet him face to face.

Terry Burns is an agent with Hartline Literary Agency as well as writing inspirational fiction and over 400 articles and short stories. As a writer he has over 40 books in print including 10 novels. A bookstore of his available works and a regular blog can be found at www.terryburns.net.

Christine Callaway

MURDERER!

THE PEW WAS uncomfortable and unfamiliar. When was the last time I sat in a church pew? Regardless of how long it has been, I was now in church, a place I did not want to be.

"Murderer! What right do you have to be in God's house?"

I thought whoever said those words spoke them loud enough for the whole congregation to hear. Yet no one was looking around to see who the accusation was addressed to, or where it came from. But I knew. It was me. There was only one other person who knew my secret - God. Was He my accuser? Were those words really spoken out loud?

I wanted to run as fast as I could down the aisle and out the doors, away from the church and everyone inside. But I couldn't. Running would draw attention to me, and the last thing I wanted or needed was to be noticed. I also knew that if I walked, let alone ran, I would never come back.

Was I really a murderer? I had never called myself that, but I did admit that she was dead, and I was to blame. What right did I have to be in church? None! So for years I not only stayed away from the church, but from God.

I stood when everyone else stood, mouthing the words to familiar hymns. When it came time for the sermon, I obediently opened my Bible to the passages the chaplain directed, as my mind drifted back to the events leading up to her death.

I had just graduated from high school and my dad, an Air Force sergeant, was being transferred for the third time in as many years. I was in no hurry to go to the next base, so I decided to visit my grandparents before starting college. Little did I know that by staying behind, not only would my faith be tested, but I would be responsible for her death.

Two weeks into the visit, my grandmother was hospitalized. Feeling helpless I did the only thing I knew to do. I prayed, and like so many others, I made a deal with God. "God, if you let her live I will..."

Who was I to make a deal with God? A deal is an agreement between two people, yet I was the one dictating the terms. A few days after my grandmother came home, it was time to start thinking about joining my parents and enrolling in college. The promise was forgotten!

A week later I was back, attending her funeral. Walking out of the church, I overhead my great-uncle say, "Had Chris not left, she would still be alive." I couldn't believe my ears! Did he really believe that I was responsible for her death?

My uncle's careless words, spoken during a moment of grief, haunted me for years to come. Those words, plus my own guilt began to destroy not only my faith, but my relationship with God.

Coming back to the present, I realized the choir was singing, and soon the service would end. Staring at the open Bible in my hand, I knew I had to stop blaming myself for my grandmother's death. I also needed to forgive my uncle for the careless words he spoke through his pain.

Forgiving my uncle was the first and easiest step on my journey to wholeness. The self-blaming for my grandmother's death came to an end as God's Word, "Therefore, there is now no condemnation, for those who are in Christ Jesus" (Romans 8:1), began to take root in the soul of my heart. Today I walk in freedom no longer a victim of my own self-imposed guilt.

Christine Callaway is a certified life-purpose coach and a health and wellness coach whose articles and stories have been published in various magazines and books. A CLASS graduate, Chris has spoken at schools and at women's events and retreats throughout the country. She lives in Arizona with her mother.

Judi Clarke

Dad Knows

I WAS AS gloomy as the weather. We wound our way down the highway hugging Alaska's spectacular mountains on one side and the silty gray waters of Turnagain Arm on the other. Skies were thick with clouds and it was raining, again. This would very likely be our only chance to visit Alaska and I was disappointed that so many of our days were filled with such dreary skies. It was early in our marriage and finances were tight. But because we had a friend who'd recently moved to Anchorage, we had a free place to stay, a truck we could borrow, and our own private tour guide. If we ever wanted to visit Alaska we needed to seize this opportunity.

Due to work restrictions for the summer months, our trip was planned for September. My husband worked extra jobs to earn the money. Saving what we could, funds still fell short. We resorted to the credit card to make up what was lacking in savings.

We were so excited to be in Alaska. The magnitude of its beauty thrilled us. Yet here I was on this one particular day, in a sour mood because of the weather. What was really gnawing at me underneath was guilt. As we drove along in yet another rain, it all came crashing together inside me and I blurted out, "God's probably giving us all this rain because we didn't do this trip right and had to use our credit card!"

Thus was my relationship with God at that time. While we do have a responsibility to live within our income, my comment revealed I was living with a God who I thought was always standing over me, watching and waiting for me to mess up, and ready to punish me when I did. A God eager to express His displeasure and disappointment in me, a God who's love and favor I had to earn by my good behavior. My husband reminded me God isn't like that. He doesn't punish us for our mistakes or even our sins. There is no more condemnation for Christians. (Romans 8:1) He died for all of it already. I still felt so wrong and guilty that the truth my husband spoke didn't even sink in. I continued to believe the theology preached to me by my guilt.

Eight years later we decided to take an early 10-year anniversary trip back to Alaska. Magnificent beauty accompanied us on our drive north to Denali Park, home of Mt. McKinley. Gorgeous mountains, forests, and lush meadows surrounded us. Mountain ranges rose above tranquil lakes reflecting their perfect images on the still waters. It was breathtaking. During one stretch of road we remained quiet, lost in our own thoughts absorbing the beauty. My thoughts led me to all the lush grass we were driving past and I commented on how beautiful it was. I followed up my marveling with, "I wonder how many blades of grass there are in the world." A silly rhetorical thought born out of the wonder of creation.

My husband marveled back that it would be utterly impossible to know. Before he could put the period on his sentence, my thoughts said to me, "Dad knows!" The words caught my mental breath. I thought to myself, "Wow! I just referred to God as 'Dad.'" I was struck with how immediate, how natural yet unexpected it was. A smile grew on my face as I savored this sweet and special moment. Dad knows. *Dad* knows! I will forever hold in my heart that simple, spontaneous inner sentence. What a difference from eight years earlier when I thought God was punishing us with rain because we hadn't financed our vacation wisely. Rain and clouds, in *Alaska* of all places! Just where did I think all that lushness came from anyway? Dad knows.

Judi Clarke lives with her husband in Arizona in an off-grid cabin they built with their own hands. She has struggled with fear most of her life and now helps others move from fear to a deep and trusting relationship with God through her blog www.fear2eternity.blogspot.com.

Charlotte Riegel

God's Protection

SHE CAME TO us from another city through a pregnancy support agency. She was here to wait out the weeks till her baby was past the safe period for a surgical abortion. Claire, a teenager, wanted to keep the baby, but her boyfriend and mother hounded her to get rid of it, so she ran away. We quickly learned of her street savvy intelligence gleaned from occasional nights in abandoned vehicles. It did not take her long to make friends with the local bar crowd.

I was totally convinced she would have one bang up house party during our weekend attendance at a function six hours away. Although I trusted her, I did not trust her friends. Prior to our Friday departure she headed off to temporary employment at a nearby daycare centre. Just before leaving for our trip I walked around our old mobile home, filled with hand-me-downs and garage sale specials, praying, "God, please protect our home while we are away. It's not much, but it's all we have." I also asked God to confuse Claire's plans for a party. Then we left.

Weekend events kept my mind occupied and I didn't think about our home until we drove onto our yard. "I wonder what we will find," I said to my husband.

"Well, the outside looks just fine. Stop fretting," he chided.

I was not prepared for what I saw entering the kitchen. Nothing had changed since our departure. This seemed most unusual because Claire enjoyed being in the kitchen, cooking and helping with meal cleanup. I had left a few dirty dishes in the sink and they were just as I had left them. Walking through the rest of the house it appeared absolutely nothing had been moved or changed. It felt eerie. Claire was not home. The tranquility of the situation confused me.

A few hours later a telephone call informed us she had been taken to the hospital by her employer on Friday, before we ever left town. "I have a kidney infection. The doctors say I can leave here in a day or two. I'll call you to pick me up when they give the okay," she said. Hanging up the phone, I stood in stunned amazement and gratitude as I realized my prayer for God's protection had been answered...not the way I'd imagined, but in His perfect way.

Charlotte Riegel lives with her husband, Stanley, in Calgary, Alberta, Canada. They are blessed with five adult children and 10 grandchildren. Their home, Bridge of Hope, has housed many people in distress or in life transition. The Riegels are actively involved at Centre Street Church.

Laura Krämer

FEASTING WITH THE ENEMY

IT COMES OFTEN, stays too long, and wreaks havoc on my heart. Even still, I welcome disappointment into my home and heart. As much as this is a part of life, I have the tendency to invite this seemingly charming friend to sit and have coffee with me. I visit into the wee hours of the morning and drink in my right to commiserate.

Over the years my coffee time with this gloomy friend has evolved into a five-course feast. I invite my girlfriends to the feast as despair takes the place of honor. We all partake with the belief it will nourish us. Somehow we are always grateful for the generous dessert disappointment brings to the feast. It dishes out victim mentalities with a refill of pity parties in our cups.

I wonder how many feasts I have given over the years in honor of disappointment...

I remember a time when unhappiness came knocking on my door again. My husband failed to meet my expectations. While at a conference, I felt out of my comfort zone. I called home to share my anxieties. My husband was too busy to talk and felt disappointed.

Who can I invite to my feast? Friends had long stopped accepting my invitations. I resigned to sit down for coffee with this hopelessness by myself. Slowly, I began to drink in my pity party. My spirit paused. I put the cup down. I was suddenly aware of the bitterness of my soul.

The bitterness left an aftertaste that lingered for days. As each day came and went, I saw more and more the condition of my heart. To my surprise, it had not been nourished with the many feasts at all. My heart clearly suffered from malnutrition. The very thing I thought was good for me only caused damage. I could now understand why eating the fruit of blaming others never made me feel better, but instead caused a vicious cycle of entertaining displeasure.

I began to grieve the state of my heart. More and more the horrible taste of pity parties, blaming others, and victim mentality filled my mouth.

And then it struck me. I have made my life to be about me. I fell to my knees.

"Lord, I'm sick of me. I'm sick of the poor ways I handle disappointment, the places in my heart I keep away from You. I blame You for things I shouldn't. I keep doing the same stupid stuff, thinking it will turn into something good. I'm so sick of me."

"Come to Me," I heard Him say.

He asked for my cup. I willingly gave it to Him. He tossed the cup farther than I could see. He gave me His cup filled with living water.

"Drink it in," He said.

I couldn't drink it fast enough. I had never tasted anything so sweet. I felt His living water fill me with His love, grace, and mercy. I felt my heart regain its health. Strength was returned and with it renewed clarity of vision. In gratitude I extended the Lord's cup back to Him.

"It is yours," He said.

Feeling unworthy I looked at His cup and for the first time saw it to be a royal crystal goblet gleaming with jewels. My heart sank. How could I receive His gift after years of feasting with the enemy? Most of the entrées served at the feast were my unrealistic expectations for my husband. How could I possibly keep this undeserved gift?

"Keep it," He said.

I looked again at His gift. Tears splashed on the crystal rim. Each one became gold as it hit the goblet. My tears of confession revealed a renewed identity. I am a forgiven daughter of the King. This is the identity I am meant to drink from. No longer will I drink from a victim's cup, but rather from a victorious one.

Gone are the days of drinking in misery with the enemy. Instead I drink in contentment with my King. He fills my cup. A generous overflow of gentleness and kindness spills onto friends and family. They come expectantly to the feast. The Lord takes His place of honor. Together we feast on gladness from our Lord as I serve my husband a large helping of respect.

Laura Krämer is a speaker, writer, and designer of The Psalm 23 Bracelet. Featured in numerous national and local publications, her design has sold in over 35 nations. Laura's passion is leading others closer to the heart of God. She lives in Southern California with her husband and two boys.

Roger Ross

Working Clay

I CAN'T GO on like this," I told my spiritual director. "Something in my life has got to change. I'm putting everything up on the table: my job, my career, the direction of my life, everything. I am going to stay married to my wife and be a father to my kids, but everything else is up for grabs."

I had come to the retreat broken. The betrayal of a close co-worker coupled with an inhuman schedule had scorched my soul. My trust meter was at an all-time low. And although I didn't know it, I blamed God.

My spiritual director suggested forms of prayer that would get me out of my head. The retreat offered a session for praying with clay, so I took it. One by one the instructor plopped a cold lump of clay in front of us and said, "Now, let the clay become what it wants to be."

Right, I grumbled to myself, *You have got to be kidding*. But I was desperate. My prayers had long since run out of words that meant anything. My heart had grown cold. Maybe doing something that felt this silly would unlock some forgotten door.

As I worked the clay in my hands, it got softer and warmer. At first I shaped things that were my ideas—a cross, a boat, the Empire State Building. (OK, that was a stretch.) But I was missing the point. So I balled up the clay and tried very hard not to make anything.

While pushing and pulling this lifeless lump, it took an unexpected form. It looked like my hand. Just then the class came to an end. I thought, *That's it?* Bewildered and disappointed, I took my "masterpiece" back to my room and put it on the bed stand.

Two days later I wrestled with God in complete silence. Over an hour passed with nothing to show for it—no word, no peace, no hint that God was even there. Out of this darkness, an image emerged in my mind's eye. A mass of multi-colored clay was turning and twisting at a rapid pace. I didn't know what to make of it. Suddenly, out of the center of the undulating clay came two words in large block letters: TRUST ME. A moment later, it was gone.

The whole experienced lasted less than five seconds, but for the first time in many months, I knew God had not abandoned me. Quite the opposite, God was at work deep below the surface of my soul. Underneath my spiritual flat line, God was doing something I could neither see nor know. This was the invitation: *Trust Me.*

Trust Me that it will turn out alright, that I have it under control, and that I love you more than you can know.
Trust Me that you are in the palm of my hand, that I will make your heart soft and warm again, and that you are being formed for a new purpose.
Trust Me. Stop struggling. It's OK.
Just Trust Me.

I did.

As a pastor, speaker, and writer, Roger's two great passions in life are connecting the spiritually unconnected with Jesus Christ and seeing transformed churches transform the world. Roger is married to Leanne Klein Ross, and they have two incredible children, Zach and Jane. He also has a weakness for golf.

Anne Arvizu

HOME AGAIN?

THE MOURNFUL SILENCE in the car was broken by the sound of large tear drops thudding against the leather seats of our Mercedes. We had just come out of our final failed business development attempt in Miami. Another miscommunication, and more ideas spilled out on people who had no intention of using our services. My husband's tears were a signal that our small business had flatlined and we had to seek employment. It was almost Christmas, and we had started sinking into debt.

By mid February, we were there. Each dollar spent dug us deeper in, but my husband took his valentines out to lunch. As we ordered the least expensive sandwiches and contemplated which slice of cheesecake to split with our oldest daughter, Love called to say hello. An HR representative rang with good tidings, telling us of my husband's new job. We knew we had to move, but the financial crisis was almost over. We all ate cheesecake that day.

Reeling but relieved, the clumsy process of relocating from Florida to Pennsylvania commenced in March. Jaime's first paycheck arrived just as we were on our last cash-out of 401K. In this whirlwind, we lost all we had and we moved to the one place on earth I didn't want to go. My personal Nineveh, circa my childhood home: Collegeville, PA. Over the summer and fall months, we plodded along and settled in. Like Job, we were able to mourn a bit, stay on our knees, and worship. We navigated our new normal and an uneventful year of work and ministry slipped away. In the darkest, coldest months of winter we learned Jaime's company was going to be sold. Twenty thousand people were slated to lose their jobs. That's when we started to find the pennies again.

The first time I found one two years earlier, I had just headed out for a sunny early morning worship walk before wrestling the piles of bills and work on my desk. iPod cranked up, I picked up a hot little glimmer of hope in a seemingly bleak situation. I held it as if this one coin completed me. As our clients decreased the pennies increased. We couldn't try to look for them, they found us. We rejoiced each time we found these copper beacons which simply stated, 'In God We Trust.' We thanked Him for the income and taught our kids to do the same. We gathered a bucketful of pennies over that year and tithed from them. With jingling pockets and joyful hearts, we pressed on knowing we were never alone. When the pennies started again in Pennsylvania, we knew it was a sign change was coming but it was nothing to fear. "God you brought us this far," we prayed in faith, "you are not going to leave us now. We don't know what you have planned, but it certainly includes provision."

As the year passed, pink slips were abundantly littered through Jaime's company. Jaime's office became a chapel for those who wondered why he was so cheerful. He'd ask them if they had ever read Psalm 91. "Ten thousand will fall at my side but it will not come near me." Finally, this January, we got two relocation offers. In this dark time, when thousands are out of work, Jaime was offered two jobs.

A promotion in New York in his company or a lesser job, a demotion in title and salary, back in Fort Lauderdale. With prayer, confirmation and wise counsel, we recognized God's fingerprint all over the Florida opportunity. God was sending us home. Because Jaime turned down the NY job, God's favor provided us a generous unexpected severance package people only with five to ten years tenure received. In one day, our entire losses were restored.

So many adversaries. Two years and two cross country moves. The death of my mother-in-law, my schnauzer and our business and the birth of my website and full time ministry launch. We have lived in five places total, sold and bought two houses, been uprooted, unsettled and up in the air. And we wouldn't change a thing. I bet Jesus would say the same thing if you asked him about the road to Calvary. God is well able to do exceedingly abundantly above all we could ask or think and He is still in the restoration, relocation, and resurrection business today.

Founder of Christian Coaching International, (www.GodCoach.com), Anne Arivizu empowers leaders to achieve the GodDream™ within. Challenging believers to walk in a manner worthy of their calling, Dr. Arvizu sees tripping stones as foundations, mountains as a means to rise above, and oceans as an opportunity to walk on water.

Evelyn Gutierrez

Greater is He

BRIGHT LIGHT SPILLED in from one end of the tunnel. As I went toward it, I heard weeping coming from the other direction. I turned to see my family sitting in what seemed to be a waiting room. I froze, suspended somewhere between the two.

"MOM!" I stretched my hands out as far as I could reach. "Mom? Dad?" Why couldn't they hear me? Men in white coats huddled around my parents. The muffled sounds of conversation echoed down through the tunnel. I couldn't make out the words.

"Please! Somebody tell me what's going on!" No matter what I said, no one budged. My knees buckled. I slunk to a heap in the middle of the tunnel and began to repeat the Scripture Mom always used to encourage me in times of trouble. "Greater is He that is in me than He that is in the world" (1 John 4:4).

Minutes drifted by. I sat. Muffled conversation intensified. I heard beeping, some yelling, and then a long high-pitched sound. The pull of the Light strengthened. I couldn't bring myself to get up.

Helpless, I watched as my mom screamed and threw herself into Dad's arms. Whatever those men said must be pretty bad. "Say the verse with me, Mom, say the verse. Greater is He that is . . ."

Dad's voice interrupted my thought. "How could this happen? Yesterday she was helping me at the shelter, and today . . ."

"Dad? Dad! I'm OK!" I tried again to get Dad's attention, but my words came out muddled, like I had a mouthful of marbles. The next I knew, both Mom and Dad stood over me, their hot tears splashing on my face.

"Honey, look! She's trying to tell us something!" Mom cried harder, and I nodded the best I could with tubes taped every which way across my face. I felt disoriented and very confused. Again, I tried to talk, but I couldn't. Dad put a pencil in my left hand and slid a pad of paper under my wrist. I'm right-handed, but I wrote the best I could.

Why are you crying?

What happened?

What's wrong?

A smile replaced Mom's tears. "There's nothing wrong with her! She's already asking questions!"

Doctors soon declared my recovery a miracle. I'd been in a coma for nearly four weeks.

Dad later explained that I had died on the table during surgery to remove a blood clot from my lung. "But one of the doctors wouldn't give up. He just kept working and working until finally your heart started beating again.

"They came into the waiting room and told us what happened. 'Mr. and Mrs. Baca,' he said, 'your daughter is alive, but she's suffered sever brain damage. She will never have a normal life.'"

A vegetable. No hope of a normal life. They didn't know the love and power of my God. Though it was impossible for man, God raised me from among the dead. He wasn't done with me yet. His plans for me didn't include lying in bed being fed through a tube for the rest of my life. "With God, all things are possible" (Matthew 19:26). To Him be the glory!

Now, years later, I'm still grateful to God for the gift of my life and the ability to love the poor from the overflow of His love and mercy. I continue the ministry begun by my father, serving thousands of meals to the homeless in Albuquerque, New Mexico, through the Tomas Baca Food Pantry.

Evelyn Gutierrez is a book table volunteer for the CLASS Christian Writers Conference for three years. She has managed the Tomas Baca Food Pantry for the last 15 years. When not volunteering she provides daycare for her grandchildren. Evelyn and her husband Gilbert have two daughters.

Matt Andrews

GOD'S OUTPOURING

IT'S BEEN A long day already, so I'm hesitant to open my email. I find the "check mail" button often acts as a closed door in an abandoned house. Behind it could be treasure or skeletons, but there's no way to know without turning the door knob.

First email: A collage of kitten photos, a Bible verse, and rambling thoughts about love. At the end of it I read that if I *truly* love Jesus, I'll take the time to *forward* the email to TEN MORE PEOPLE. I decide that if I *really* love those ten people, I will *delete* these kittens and serve Jesus another way.

Second email: A simple note from Steven, a student in my youth group, saying thank you for a difficult but necessary phone conversation. I smile, because in youth ministry a little encouragement goes a long way.

Third email: I swore I heard a ticking time bomb when I opened my inbox, and here it is. Subject line: *Urgent Prayer Request*. I see from the header that Steven's mother has written and forwarded this to everyone in our church. The "prayer request" turns out to be an embarrassing list of her son's recent failures—followed by a plea: "Pray that the Lord will send our church a youth leader who can *properly* train our children."

I stare at the computer screen, trying to suppress the urge to hit "reply" and publicly voice a few thoughts about *her*. I wonder: What's going on in her mind that would make her do this?

It doesn't take me long to remember that, for both of us, the problem is not in our *heads*, but our *hearts*. Jesus is clear: *Out of the "overflow" of the heart the mouth speaks.*

Later in the day I take a walk and, in spite of the hours that have passed the overflow from *my* heart percolates black and sticky. I reach a truce with my spirit: Even though I can't stop my heart from overflowing with evil intent, I think I *can* keep my mouth shut.

Before I reach the end of the block my plan hits a snag. My neighbor Rose calls out, "Hello," her smile sagging from some obvious pain. I nod, consumed by my own predicament; she returns to watering her lawn. But I've been involved in ministry long enough to know she needs something—an attentive ear, or maybe a *word* of hope.

I look at Rose's garden hose soaking the dry blades of grass, grass that never seems to get enough water. A scripture comes to mind: "In the beginning was the Word, and the Word was with God, and the Word was God" (John 1:1 NASB). A few more steps and another phrase haunts me: "Then God said, 'Let there be light,' and there was light" (Genesis 1:3 NASB).

This is the power of the Living Word-speaking life into existence. I know the words that overflow from me, as a follower of Christ, should also bring life. But in my bitterness I bring rocks to throw in revenge, then silence, which in its own way hurts more than sticks and stones.

I turn back.

I open my mouth.

I'm afraid of what I'll say, but I pray it will help.

I trust through the overflow of His Forgiveness *of* me, God pours *from* me something good, healing and pleasing.

Matt Andrews wasted time figuring out what he wanted. Then, he spent three years working with (and learning from) the homeless of San Francisco's Tenderloin district with his wife, Kristi. He has a bachelor's degree in theology from Colorado Christian University. His marriage and two children are his favorite accomplishments.

Pam Farrel

LIFE FROM DEATH - GOD'S PARADOX OF BLESSING

"I tell you the truth, unless a kernel of wheat falls to the ground and dies, it remains only a single seed. But if it dies, it produces many seeds."

—John 12:24

PICTURE MY LIFE as a beautiful, hand-crocheted afghan. There are many interwoven threads creating this work of art. Bill, the senior pastor of the largest church in our city, had just moved our congregation into a beautiful new building. Our book, *Men are like Waffles, Women are like Spaghetti,* hit the bestsellers' list. Our teens were making great choices. The church was growing, as was our writing and speaking for marriages and families. We thought, *Life just doesn't get any better than this!* Then, it was as if someone grabbed hold of one thread and our lives began to unravel.

One day, we were traveling, doing media appearances, and Bill wasn't feeling well, so he went to the doctor. His blood pressure was spiking erratically. This news got our attention, because Bill's grandfather died of a stroke at age 47 and his father had a stroke that left him disabled at age 48. Bill was 45. The doctor asked about his life, "Got any stress?" When Bill described his mountain of responsibility, the physician replied, "Bill, you are a people helper. What would you tell someone who came into your office displaying these symptoms?"

Bill replied, "You have some strategic decisions to make." Exactly. So, to make a very long, painful story shorter, Bill ended up resigning from the church he'd pastored for over 15 years. While we purposely slowed Bill's pace, I felt my own tension grow. We were trying to keep one kid in college and prepare for another's send-off for his education, all while more money was flowing out of our bank account than into it.

One week in particular sticks out to me. Our youngest was hit illegally in a football game, rushed to Children's Hospital with internal bleeding and given a blood transfusion.

He was in ICU for eight days. When we brought Caleb home, I had a speaking engagement that the family needed me to keep. The first night, our middle son, Zach, was pulled from his football game with a concussion and knee injury, putting his chances for a college scholarship at risk. The next night, Brock, our oldest, a Junior College quarterback, was pulled from the game with what we thought might be a career-ending shoulder injury. Sunday, my sister-in-law called with the news that my 40-year-old brother had experienced a heart attack, and she asked if I could care for her kids. (Other than that, Mrs. Lincoln, how'd you like the theater?) I prayed in desperation, *Lord, who am I supposed to save first?*

One morning, I sat in a friend's church when the Spirit reminded me of John 12:24, "...unless a seed falls to the ground and dies...." I prayed, DIES! Lord, I don't want our dream to die! The Spirit reminded me of part B of the verse: "but if it dies, it produces many seeds." You are right, Lord. The dream is dead and buried. By faith, we anticipate the new harvest You have for us.

I printed out all the verses on God's goodness, favor, and blessing. I prayed Job 42 over our future—that God would give us more in the second half of life than in the first. Joyce Meyer says of Job that God gave "double for his trouble." By faith, I awaited God's provision. However, I just didn't know how to reply when people would ask, "So, how are you doing?" The answer was too long, too personal, or too depressing. Often, when asked, we moan, "Well, pretty good under the circumstances." I love Professor Howard Hendricks' response, "Under the circumstances? What are you doing under there?"

I began to ask God, "How shall I answer these well-meaning friends?" I felt God simply whisper a question to my heart, "What kind of woman do you want to be, Pam?" *Lord, I want to be the kind of person who can choose joy whatever life sends her way. Your Word says, 'The joy of the Lord is our strength,' (Nehemiah 8:10), and we need strength right now!* As a result, I decided my new answer would be, *"Choosin' joy!"*

I chose joy, day after day, and then, one by one, God began to send blessings of speaking engagements, book contracts, and renewed health for Bill accompanied by a staff pastoral position with Dr. David Jeremiah. Both older sons garnered college scholarships, and our eldest married a beautiful, godly wife. God gave more than double for our trouble. It took about three years, but overflowing joy and blessings arrived—the promised harvest!

Pam Farrel is an international speaker, relationship expert, and author of over 30 books including the best-selling *Men Are Like Waffles, Women Are Like Spaghetti*. She is co-director of Love-Wise (www.love-wise.com) as well as Seasonedsisters.com, a ministry of hope and help for women over 40.

David Cary

GOD'S GOODNESS

NO ONE LIKES unpleasant surprises in life, especially the kind where your whole life comes skidding to a halt.

My health had been excellent for quite some time. Work was pressing, but manageable. Church involvements took their routine place on weeknights and weekends. Family time included Sunday noon meals, hang-out time and travel. Frequent trips to the gym involved rigorous workouts. Life was good.

One evening after a trip to the gym, I told my wife I didn't feel well. Thinking it was a typical bug, I took some Airborne and went to bed. I awoke the next morning with a headache and fever. By evening, my body was one big ache and the fever was a persistent 103 degrees, not responding to any fever reducers.

Over the next two weeks, I went to the doctor twice and the emergency room once, but found no relief. As my liver and kidneys malfunctioned, I became disoriented and confused. In desperation, my caring wife took me back to our family doctor and told him with a hint of humor, "I'm not sure what can be done to help him, but, I'm not taking him back home!"

I was admitted to the hospital that night and the testing began. Spinal tap, X-rays, MRI's, CAT scans, bone scans, bone marrow test—64 vials of blood were drawn over eleven days. Three different antibiotics were administered in hopes something would help—one so potent it blew out the veins in both hands. The fever persisted. My body was extremely weak. I tired emotionally of all the poking and prodding.

I started hurling questions God's way: "Lord, why is this happening? Where are you? Is this really a part of your plan for my life? Is your plan that I should leave this world at the young age of 51? I need to hear something from you!" I didn't hear any answers, and I was discouraged.

I picked up a card on the bed stand, opened it, and found a Scripture reference handwritten at the bottom. Not knowing what the Scripture said, I looked it up and found the exhortation, "Wait for the Lord; be strong and take heart and wait for the Lord" (Psalm 27:14). I hashed the thought over several times during the next couple of days. Though I considered this verse a word from the Lord and began to take heart, I still felt fear and was void of hope.

Word came that the illness might be a super virus called Cytomegalovirus (CMV). My wife did some research and found this could be very serious, causing blindness, organ damage—even death. Though she didn't tell me the full extent of the threat, I could see the concern on her face as she visited with the doctors.

God saw my need for more assurances and responded a second time. He drew my attention to the verse right before the one that had instructed me to be strong: "I am still confident of this: I will see the goodness of the Lord in the land of the living" (Psalm 27:13). I connected with this thought and began to feel at peace. Whether "the land of the living" was on earth or in heaven, I knew I could count on the goodness of the Lord.

Eventually the tests confirmed it was the CMV virus. I breathed a sigh of relief as the doctors told me my body would develop its own antibodies and I would heal in four to six months. Soon after, the blood work showed my liver and kidneys were beginning to heal. This meant I was being spared any serious damages.

Regaining my health is a miracle, but learning to focus on God's goodness gives hope for the rest of my life. When I suffer in the future, I am confident I will continue to see the goodness of the Lord.

David Cary has experience in business, ministry, and psychotherapy. He has a Bachelor of Arts degree from Kansas City College and Bible School. He has served in various roles in ministry including pastor, district superintendent, writer, and radio speaker. David and his wife Holley live in Bartlett, TN.

Robin Stanley

EVERY LIFE FOR GOOD

"HE DIDN'T MAKE it."

The sting of my brother's words scattered my thoughts. The birth of his son, William Steven Stanley, came a month too soon.

He separated from his life source. No warning. No shout from his cozy growing space. His active body simply stopped. No one knows why. But we do know the sting is real. Losing life hurts. When life ends, grief grows toward a season of sorrow. And sorrow mingles among the tears of the living, weaving its way through a family, a community.

When God set loose his breath within this tiny human form and provided parents for his nurturing and protection, he intended for good.

He intends every life for good.

My brother grapples for understanding as he attempts to dismantle the beginnings of a nursery. "We saw the baby clap his hands. The nurse doing the ultrasound said that maybe he would grow up to be a gospel singer. No matter what she did, he just kept clapping." His voice trailed off. "Now I can't get this - this crib thing apart. I just put it together. You'd think I could figure it out."

Silence spilled into the air, stopping short our conversation. Jim hung up, and my heart broke.

Oh, God, I feel his hurt. His struggle with the finite nature of the human body. His frustration with not being able to make things better. Please reveal Yourself to him in his grief. Show him a resurrected life from this tragic death.

It had been a year since the last time I saw Jim. As we gathered around our great Aunt Pearle who suffered a severe stroke, I saw firsthand his tearful journey with sorrow.

When I entered her room, Jim looked up from the foot of her bed. Tears poured out his helplessness. "She's not going to make it." I wrapped my arms around his neck. We cried together. She didn't make it.

At her funeral, we found a way to express our love and celebrate the impact of her long life. We remembered sitting on the steps while she told of her travels, pointing at a different saltshaker for every state she'd been in. We marveled at the way she brought life to those around her, even from a wheelchair when she broke a hip and couldn't be her normal bustling self.

God intends every life for good.

When Jim called to tell me about his son, I wanted to wrap my arms around his neck and cry together. I know it wouldn't make his hurt go away. I don't want to make his hurt go away. Only God can do that. But I would sit with him in his sorrow. I would celebrate with him the short life of his stillborn son. And I would help him see how the sorrow in his and Cheryl's tears and Mom's and Dad's tears and my tears and his friend's tears mingle together to validate that life—a life that God intends for good.

A connector and communicator, Robin Stanley comes alongside writers and worshipers ready to yield their life stories and purposes to God. She offers a safe place for discerning and distributing their God-given gifts through Christ-centered, relationship-based coaching and representation. A member of the CLASSEMINARS, Inc. board of directors and founder of o3-free, Robin is a mentor, a worshiper, a traveler, a friend.

Daina Doucet

Too Young for a Heart Attack

IT WAS EARLY Sunday morning, and I was getting ready for church when the phone rang. My son-in-law was on the line. "Kenda's having severe chest pains," he said in an even tone. "I've got the kids at home. Can you drive her to emergency? I think you should hurry."

I was surprised at the calmness in his voice. My mind raced as I hung up the phone. *She can't be having a heart attack*, I thought. *She's healthy and fit. She doesn't smoke. She doesn't drink. She eats right. She's only 27—and she's 14 weeks pregnant. The baby! What about the baby?*

I grabbed the keys, flew out the door, and drove around the block to their house. I found her in the living room sprawled on the couch, her face drawn and pasty white. She teetered forward as her husband helped her up. He lifted her and carried her down the stairs. Their two little girls, Mekiah, four years old, and Jada, two, stood sobbing at the door as mommy left.

Kenda lay in the passenger seat panting in shallow gasps. It occurred to me that we might not make it to the hospital, even though it is only five minutes from our house in Hamilton, Ontario. Just then, I felt the familiar, gentle presence of God's Spirit. I lay one hand on Kenda's arm, steered the car with the other, and prayed.

When we arrived at the hospital, an ambulance pulled into the spot to the left of us. As I glanced at it, something like a wave washed over me. Words and images that weren't there before rushed into my mind in an instant download. Feeling as if I were following a script, I called to the ambulance driver, "Do you have anyone in there? My daughter is having chest pains."

The driver came around to the passenger side and exchanged a few muffled words with her. "Go get a chair," he told the attendant who had accompanied him. Moments later, overwhelmed by the extraordinary favor, I followed the attendant through the sliding doors, past admitting, past triage, and past the patients pacing and sitting in the reception area. It was as if the Red Sea parted. Kenda proceeded directly into an examining room. In the five minutes it took me to register her, she was on a stretcher and attached to a cardiac monitor that confirmed a heart attack.

Kenda spent the next ten days hooked to a wall of monitors in the cardiac intensive care unit. The cardiologist had identified a blood clot in her heart. "You picked the best hospital in Canada to come to," he assured her. "We specialize in pregnancy-related heart problems." We shared both the diagnosis and the story of God's amazing intervention with our church family who immediately prayed.

During that time, several medical professionals impressed upon us the significance of her quick admission. "It's a miracle," they said. "Had she not been admitted by an ambulance attendant within 15 minutes from the onset of the heart attack, the consequences could have been fatal."

But we were not out of the wilderness yet. The doctors still had considerable concern for the baby. The ultrasound didn't look good. The baby had cysts on the brain and problems with the heart—signs of Down's syndrome or worse—potentially stillbirth. In addition, the blood flow in the umbilical cord was so restricted that the baby would have to be delivered at the end of the second trimester. Again, friends began to pray. We experienced a groundswell of support. Entire churches undertook on our behalf, and we received encouragement through phone calls and e-mail messages from complete strangers.

Two weeks later Kenda returned for her scheduled appointment. The doctor looked bewildered as he compared ultrasound images. "That's strange," he said. "We had our best technician on it the last time, and I'm sure we didn't make a mistake. The cysts have disappeared and the blood flow in the umbilical cord seems to be normal now. How's that possible?"

It may not have been possible medically, but nothing is impossible with our Father in heaven (Luke 1:37). Even though Kenda was still deemed high-risk, Aliyah was born on March 6, 2003—a perfect, miracle baby.

As I recount this story, I marvel again at the wonder of God's extraordinary presence in our ordinary lives and thank Him for His family whose prayers defeat the impossible.

Daina Doucet edits Christianity.ca for The Evangelical Fellowship of Canada. She is a freelance writer and book editor formerly employed with Crossroads Christian Communications and Toronto Airport Christian Fellowship. Daina has contributed to numerous publications including Faith & Friends, Faith Today, Ministries Today, and Charisma.

Gerry Wakeland

FILL MY CUP, LORD!

I WENT INTO my office and closed the door. I sat down at my desk, buried my head in my hands and cried out to God. "I am so tired, so empty," I said. It had been a tough few months and ministry had taken its toll on my body and my spirit.

Almost immediately God responded with a picture. It was a measuring cup much like the Pyrex kind most women keep in their kitchens. In my case it was the four-cup size. I could even see the red markings along the side of the cup.

Then God began to speak to me, not in an audible voice but in that Spirit voice that I've learned to recognize. He told me I was like that measuring cup. I poured from my cup into many people and events. I poured into my husband and my marriage, my children, my extended family, my neighbors, my responsibilities at the church, my friends, the women I counseled and mentored, my speaking engagements, and the list seemed to go on forever. And now here I sat empty with nothing left in my cup. "What now, Lord?" I asked.

Once again God spoke. "As you pour out, you must let me pour in," He said. I thought for a moment about what that meant, what that looked like. Another picture appeared in my mind, a picture of my empty Pyrex cup. Only this time I could see that it was being filled with a refreshing stream of water pouring down from above. It filled the cup but it did not stop. Soon the cup over flowed and spilled out. The sparkling water was splashing onto everything it came in contact with, bringing life and refreshment.

I longed for that sparkling refreshing water. How would I get it? I thought about the faucet in my kitchen at home. I thought about turning on that faucet and filling my measuring cup. That was easy. I just held the cup under the faucet and let the water fill the cup until it was overflowing. Then I realized that in order for the cup to be filled I had to stand still, intentionally holding the cup under the faucet. If I were running around the kitchen, cup in hand, the water from the faucet would simply run down the drain. Could I, would I, be still enough to let God fill my cup?

That is a question I have to ask myself over and over, day after day, as I bring my cup and hold it up for God to fill. Some days it is much easier than others. Some days the demands on my time are such that I wait only long enough to get a few drops of that sparkling water, not enough for myself let alone enough to share with others. However, on those days when I am willing to stand still or better yet to sit at His feet He is faithful to fill me. Not just to the red line at the top of my Pyrex measuring cup but He fills me until I overflow so in all I say and do I splash the joy of Jesus, the love of the Lord, and the compassion of Christ onto those around me.

Gerry Wakeland is the President and CEO of CLASSEMINARS, Inc. She loves helping Christian communicators recognize their passion, clarify their vision and define their mission so they can articulate God's message effectively. Gerry is the mother of two grown daughters and two precious grandsons and resides in the land of enchantment, Albuquerque, New Mexico. www.classeminars.org

Stephanie Rawlins

THE LOST CHILD

I WAS FATHERLESS.

By five years old, I had survived two fires. My mother, overwhelmed at the loss of our home and belongings, handed us over to the state, landing me in a New York foster home where unspeakable things happened.

By twelve years old, I was reunited with my mother. She had married a military man. Living on a military base in Texas, I remember standing at the curb in my only dress waiting for the bus to pick me up to go to church. I never knew where it would take me, Baptist, Pentecostal, Methodist, or Catholic. I felt in my heart though the church that threw wheelchairs around wasn't for me. However, I knew God was here somewhere. Why would He hide?

Why can't He find me? The Lord seemed to be an absent father, elusive.

My new step-father received orders and we left for Germany in thirty days. Once there, I discovered there wasn't a bus that came looking for those standing at the curb waiting and searching.

By sixteen, graduated from high school, my feelings were steeled. I left home that day, a home whose only commitment seemed to provide just enough food and clothing to survive. Desperate to leave, with one suitcase, my passport and a few dollars in my pocket, I walked through German security onto Lufthansa. If I was going to struggle, it had to be on home field. It had to be in the States. The Lord was written on my heart even then but a deep, scared part that was tucked away, far away.

Back in the States as a teen, I could not sign any contracts or rent a place to live. Consequently, the next years were filled with domestic violence, homelessness, poverty, and loss. Uneducated, without guidance nor mentors, somehow I still knew the Lord existed and I talked to Him from time to time.

I had to come to terms with the Lord being an absent father. Where was He to protect me and to guide me? I see now, through the years, the Lord had sent messengers. Messengers in many forms - an all girl Christian rock band who prayed over me and always with an invite to church. I politely listened but it was to late for me, just talking about church made me squirm with discomfort. Living on a military base in Texas darkness surrounded me. The Lord hadn't given up on me like I had Him. He sent more messengers, this time a Methodist minister's daughter who knew not to press or push but just live the example and patiently answer questions when I asked, another was the owner of a Christian coffee house, a Messianic Jew who showed me the "meat" in God's Word, who was obedient to the Lord yet challenged often to be shut down by the landlord. I had been running for so long, always looking over my shoulder. Then it happened, my son was born. Why was I given such an awesome gift, the wretched soul that I was? I wasn't listening for the Lord, instead He had to show me. Through my son, I came to understand unconditional love, self-sacrifice, and the responsibility to make his life safe and protected. My children were going to be raised up in the Lord whether I could find Him or not.

The Lord continued to put Christians in my path. I didn't realize He was still trying to reach me. Gradually those ladies, those messengers, guided me back to the Lord. I believed, but I was still broken. Alone one evening, filled with self-pity, crying, and babbling in prayer with questions, I heard it! Not my own words, it was a whisper that broke through the pain to simply say "I love you."

Stephanie Rawlins is a writer living in Georgetown, Texas.

Debbie Bryan

OUT OF THE BOAT

WHAT IMPOSSIBLE JOURNEY has God called you to? For me, God said to go a writers conference. In true God fashion He told me to go during a time when we barely had enough money meet our daily needs. Going involved traveling hundreds of miles, and living apart from my family for a week. The thought of going scared me. I wondered what took more faith, staying or leaving? I asked a mentor of mine for advice, and she said it was time to get out of the boat and go.

Out of the boat? Hey! There is water out there! Water in which I could sink or at the very least get wet. Sure I could get out of the boat, but might I remind you there were eleven who didn't, and Jesus loved them too. Yes, maybe there was a little envy by the others when they saw Peter go onto water. Yet when they watched him get all wet, did Peter feel it was worth it?

You want to know a secret? Like Peter, I have stepped out of that boat many times. I have kept my eyes on Christ, and I have walked and sunk over and over. I don't know what Peter was thinking that day. I do know this, he saw his Lord, and then looked away and realized his humanity and sank. His Lord didn't leave him or forsake him but pulled him up from the murky depth. That is the beauty of walking with the Lord. He never leaves you or forsakes you in the storm.

To tell the truth, I would like to be one of those eleven inside the boat. I'd grab a blanket, some food, and a DVD player and watch a chick flick or two. Then I could sit back and cheer on those suckers who dared the impossible, and still know Jesus has the power to walk on water. But I'd still be safe inside the boat. Yet, if Peter wouldn't have stepped out, the verses about that boat ride might not have been in the Bible at all. Why should they? Why was Jesus out there anyway? Was he stretching his legs or was there a reason? Maybe Christ hoped all twelve would get out of that boat, and yet just Peter, eager, thoughtless, faith-filled, overwhelmed Peter made the step.

If there is one thing I have learned about stepping out of the boat into the overflow it is that sometimes it isn't a boat at all. Sometimes your boat is a church plant, or a move, or a stay, or a call to your relative, or whatever impossible journey Christ is beckoning you to come toward. Sometimes it is even a crazy desire, like a writers conference, only fueled by a calling, and coincidences we call miracles and provision that help you make one more step without sinking. I thank God for calling me to the writers conference, and I praise Him that I stepped out of the boat and went. Even if you do fall, don't worry. Maybe that was as far as you needed to go before Christ could take your hand for the rest of the journey. Stepping out of the boat means I am walking on uncharted waters. There is only God—and isn't that enough?

Matthew 14: 28-29 "'Lord, if it's you,' Peter replied, 'tell me to come to you on the water.' 'Come,' he said. Then Peter got out of the boat and walked on the water..."

Debbie Bryan is a writer and national speaker. Her easy back porch style takes aim at everyday life with fun and insight. Debbie is a pastor's wife and mother of four. She hold's a Master's Degree in Religious Education. You can find her encouraging families, women and pastor's wives to live in God's unbounding love. Debbie can be found at marriedtoministers.blogspot.com.

Richard Osborn

The Toss of a Coin

MY ROOMMATE, DON, and I were both single, but attended different churches. One Friday night, Don asked me, "How would you like to attend my church's singles get-together at the nearby house of a fine Christian lady?"

"Sure, why not?" I replied, happy to get out of the house for the night.

I enjoyed myself among the 50-60 adult singles, but I never met the hostess—that "fine Christian lady" as Don put it.

I thought back to when I lived in Boise, Idaho, after my divorce. I spent a lot of time reading an old, tattered Tyndale *Living Bible*. One night, one verse literally jumped out at me: "We toss the coin, but it is the Lord who controls the decision" (Proverbs 16:33).

I thought about Sandy, a girl with whom I had an on-again-off-again romance. Sandy lived in California, but we kept in contact via telephone. When I saw that verse, I wondered if we would ever marry. I took a coin from my pocket and said, "OK, Lord, are Sandy and I ever going to marry? If the coin comes down heads, we will, and if it doesn't, we won't."

I tossed the coin into the air, and it came down tails. "No Lord," I said, "that's not the right answer. Let's go for two out of three." I tossed the coin into the air a second, third, even a fourth time, and it still came down tails. "Well, this is just a bunch of 'hokey' anyway."

Then my eyes glanced across the room at a *Lookout* magazine, lying on the floor. On the back cover was an advertisement for a book by Susan F. Titus entitled *Parables for Young Teens*. "Well Lord," I said, tossing the coin up again, "Who am I going to marry,

Susan F. Titus?" The coin landed heads up. "Well, that just proves this is a bunch of 'hokey.' I don't even know a Susan F. Titus." The incident was soon forgotten.

After that Friday night party, I occasionally attended Don's singles church group. I soon met a woman named Susan. One night, as a group of us were talking, Susan said, "One thing I miss from my previous marriage is the baseball tickets to the California Angels."

It just so happened I shared California Angel season tickets to box seats with a friend. I said, "Susan, I've got Angel tickets. Maybe we can go sometime." I meant this offer as only a friend, but Susan misunderstood. She cleared her throat then said quietly, "I would like to, but I am currently dating someone."

"Well," I said glibly, "if you ever change your mind, let me know."

Several months later, on a Friday night, I telephoned Sandy, and she told me she was going to marry someone else. I was shocked. I thought for sure that someday Sandy and I would marry. I never felt more alone than I did that night.

The following Sunday, Susan and I were walking from the church sanctuary to the parking lot when she stopped me and said, "Dick, remember what you said about my telling you if I ever wanted to go out with you? Well, I'd like to."

We had lunch the following Wednesday, and that evening I brought pizza to Susan's house so we could watch the winter Olympics. I was stunned when I walked into her house and realized that it was the same house that Don took me to for a get-together on that Friday night.

It didn't take long for Susan and me to become known as an item, then we became engaged. One day, while helping to carry some of Susan's son's things upstairs to his room, I noticed two framed posters hanging on the hall wall, one of which read, *Parables for Young Teens*, authored by Susan F. Titus. As I stared open-mouthed at the poster, a chill started at the top of my head and swept down to the bottom of my feet.

"Did you write that?" I asked incredulously, as Susan carried a box by me to Richard's room.

"Why, of course," she answered as she swept past, "why else would I have it hanging on my wall?"

I could not believe my eyes. Later, on our honeymoon in the Caribbean, I told Susan the story I have just told you. "But don't ever tell anyone," I said, "they'll never believe it!"

Richard Osborn has been a contractor, heavy equipment operator, paralegal, and long-haul driver. He is currently retired but helps his wife Susan keep the records for her business. He also edits her books. Dick has a 1950 restored Ford, named Henry, that he takes to car shows.

Vonda Skelton

WAIT

I HAVE A hard time waiting. I read of Sarah waiting for Isaac, Anna waiting for the Messiah, and Elizabeth waiting for John, and I'm amazed. Can you believe Sarah waited about thirty years for a baby? Thirty years? I have a hard time waiting for my nails to dry!

But God's Word is clear that we're to wait, to be still, to remain in Him:

- *Wait for the Lord; be strong and take heart and wait for the Lord. Psalm 27:14*
- *Be still before the Lord and wait patiently for him. Psalm 37:7a*
- *Remain in me, and I will remain in you. John 15:4a*

It's in the waiting that we hear God's voice. I admit there are times I can't hear God. I pray and read His Word, and yet, I don't hear a thing.

It's not His fault.

The problem is not in *His* speaking, it's in *my* listening. I have my list of prayer requests—all good things, and most are for other people. I faithfully go down the list one by one, telling God what I'd like Him to do. And then it's over. I'm off and running.

And God is left alone. There He was, just about to tell me what He wanted me to know, but I didn't have time to listen. He wanted to tell me to take the job or to turn down the volunteer position or to mentor the young bride at church. But I couldn't hear Him because I wasn't there. Because I didn't have time to wait on Him.

When I was going through a particularly unsettling time in my life, a friend shared an important step to hearing God's voice. She suggested I spend at least an hour a day just waiting on the Lord. She said two hours would be even better! Well, it took me about half a second to tell her what I thought about her great idea. Who has that kind of time? Besides, I knew exactly what would happen if I tried to do nothing but sit for an hour—I'd fall asleep!

So she told me to start small. She suggested I read Psalm 73:23 and then spend ten minutes truly meditating on the verse, listening for God's voice. I still thought she was crazy, but I told her I'd try. That first morning, I got up at 4:30, made myself a cup of coffee and settled in my chair. Taking my Bible, I read the passage and then told God I wasn't sure how to do this, but I was there, just in case He had anything He wanted to tell me.

> *Yet I am always with you; you hold me by my right hand.*
>
> —Psalm 73:23

I read the verse again and meditated on the words, *you hold me by my right hand.*

In my mind, I pictured God and me, holding hands. I sat quietly and waited.

I reread the verse and waited some more. And then I heard Him! By meditating on that one short verse and then waiting, I heard His voice! Oh, I didn't hear trumpets or receive any great revelation about my current problem, but I knew He was there. Just God and me, sitting in my chair in the corner of the living room. As He planted thoughts or single words in my mind, I pursued them, searching for another scripture that would whisper His heart.

Rest . . . wait . . . wisdom . . . peace.

I stayed with Him about an hour that first morning and longed for more. It was a new, sweet experience, one I now look forward to every morning.

I've learned to cherish our time together. And whether I have thirty minutes or an hour and a half, the time flies by. Some days I have to refocus my heart and mind again and again, and some days I hear Him more clearly than others. But I can promise you this—if I'm really there, He's really there.

It's all in the waiting. It's all in the being quiet and listening for His voice. God wants us to rest in Him. He wants to speak to our spirits and let us know He's really there. He's just waiting for us.

No agenda, no lists. Just God and me, relating to each other. I'm amazed at what He has to say when I'm quiet enough to listen.

Vonda Skelton is a national speaker, freelance writer, retired RN, and the author of four books, including *Seeing Through the Lies: Unmasking the Myths Women Believe* and the Bitsy Burroughs Mysteries for kids. She and Gary have been married 41 years—and they're still happy about it! www.VondaSkelton.com

Sonya Auston

THE FAITHFUL CALL OF GOD

CONSTANT CONFLICT, NO communication, and no chance of change described my marriage. No career, no cash, and no credit cards at my disposal described my finances. Marital problems and financial insecurity send shockwaves through the soul of any stay-at-home mom and I started to feel the impact. However, I had a promise from God.

At the age of 19 God gave me a deep passion to encourage and teach women the Word of God. Single, in a new relationship with Christ, with little knowledge of the Bible, I seemed an unlikely candidate to teach. God surrounded me with women of great faith who taught me the importance of hearing God's voice and believing His Word. I marveled as I witnessed answered prayer. In 1989 the Lord provided me with a godly husband who modeled the importance of studying God's Word consistently. Meeting the Lord in the quietness of the morning to study became my daily habit—until the children were born. My prayer became, *Lord, I am so tired this morning I have to pray lying in the bed.* Now, I laugh reminiscing about those mornings when I uttered five words, *Lord, I thank you and*... only to wake up two hours later wondering what happened.

Staying at home with my children was not my ideal of a successful career, yet it proved rewarding. Shooting basketballs, pulling boys out of kitchen cabinets, and breaking up minor skirmishes became my way of life. Praying for my children and teaching them God's Word was the highlight of my day. Watching them soak up the Scriptures and memorize verses with ease challenged me to continue studying. I began helping young mothers in my neighborhood with their daily schedules and child training. This opened up the opportunity to teach the Word of God on a weekly basis.

In 1994 a friend invited me to a women's conference featuring Florence Littauer. I was extremely intrigued with her teachings on temperament, personalities, and marriage and felt compelled to respond to what I heard. God delicately flashed memories of my past into the present. Hesitantly I handed him each memory in exchange for healing, dissolving years of confusion and pain. Joy and freedom flooded my heart the next morning, and I heard God say, "Sonya, pursue the classes offered at the conference." I gladly obeyed.

Ten years passed and our lives were extremely busy with pastoring a church, seeing people's lives changed, discipling, and raising children, while our marriage was on a fast track to destruction. I was wearied with the pain of a troubled marriage. Feeling confused, hurt, exhausted, and numb I whispered, "Father, help me, please tell me what to do."

He gently replied, "When you are ready to attend CLASS (Christian Leaders Authors Speakers Seminars) I will provide everything you need." My heart felt overwhelmed by His tenderness. I remained confident God would complete that which He began.

In May of 2010 it became evident my marriage was finished and I needed to get a job to provide for myself. Sitting at my dining room table, thoughts rolled around in my head about the difficult decisions and responsibilities I would assume. In anger I screamed, "I want to do what I love!"

God spoke. "Sonya, do not fear. I will provide for you. Do what I have called you to do." I jumped up from the chair with new life! Spending hours wondering what to do with my failing marriage, musing over hurt feelings, and contemplating angry thoughts were finished.

God has provided everything I need, just as He promised. I now fly free with two airlines criss-crossing the country. Every seminar, hotel, transportation, resources, childcare, meals, mentors, and simple pleasures have been provided for me. He continually surprises me through the faithful generosity of His people who give out of their love for him.

The conflict is calmed, communication restored, and the chances of staying married to a wonderful man are definitely on the rise. No career, no cash, and no credit cards pose no problem when you have a promise from a loving, faithful Father who will do abundantly more than all we can ask or imagine.

Sonya Auston passionately teaches women how to study the Word of God for themselves and live lives of perseverance that reflects Jesus Christ. She currently lives in the Charleston, SC area with her husband Fred. They have five amazing boys, Fred Jr., Jared, Jeremiah, Michael, and Nathaniel.

Kimberly J. Laliberte

The Relentless March

WHEN OUR SON was young, I often stood in the front yard and listened to the sounds coming from the high school down the street. I recognized the seasons by the roar of the crowd at Friday night football games, the distant sounds of cheering at Saturday morning track meets, the beat of the drum line practicing for a band competition. To me, however, the school stood in silent tribute to a future of empty nests and emotional holes.

"There is still time. Make every moment count. Pour into his soul every lesson God sends, take every opportunity to help him, 'grow in grace and knowledge'" (Luke 2:40) was often the cry of my heart as I listened. As the mother of an only child, I struggled with the thought that someday my son would not need me anymore and move on. Every June, I heard the band doggedly practicing Mendelssohn's graduation march, and even more ominous, in the summer, the sounds of the silence. Tears fell as I recognized that very soon Jonathan would take that same step. The sounds of passing time told their own stories in my life, and, as I listened to its relentless march, I grieved.

And then, I wasn't standing in the front yard merely a spectator. I was sitting on the 40-yard line and the notes of the graduation march were telling our story as it has told of countless others who went before us. Now *our* son is the graduate, straining at the bit of being forced to take photos with proud family and friends when he'd rather start his journey away from home that very night. I wasn't ready, even though for years I had prepared for the moment.

Before we knew it we were boarding an airplane to a destination 2000 miles from home, with six suitcases lining the floor waiting to be weighed-in. We apologetically explained to people in line as they stepped around our luggage, "We're moving our son to college." I could not bear to think that in six short days, I would walk away from my handsome, determined college freshman. He didn't look sad to see us go; he didn't look like I felt inside, yet I knew he would miss us. Standing strong and stoic was his gift to help us through. *Why did he have to go so far away; why couldn't he have stayed nearer?* Hillsdale College was the one and only place my son would consider. Even as I grieved the distance, I knew it fit him. We tried persuading him to stay closer to home but, in the end, had to trust God speaking to his heart.

I have found this journey particularly difficult, but also in some ways, remarkably triumphant. I am thankful I am learning to trust God's hand to reach where mine cannot. *He will not lead you where He cannot keep you,* runs through the days and nights of my mind. This is God speaking through and to our son. Jonathan loves his new life in Michigan. Is this not what we raised him for: To send him off? To let him soar with the eagles? From his days in the womb to the day we walked away from the college campus, we prayed for this man-child to grow up into all aspects of Christ Jesus—to follow where God would lead and to stand firm against anything that would entice him away from God's Truth. With millions of other parents, we are watching from the sidelines and praying from a distance. I don't really want to know about the fraternity parties or the young women he dates.

But I am thankful for Francis Thompson's poem, *The Hound of Heaven* which reminds me of God's persistence: "I fled Him, down the nights and down the days…but with unhurrying chase and unperturbed pace…" He followed. It also reminds me of God's promise to His children, "I will never leave you nor forsake you" (Hebrews 13:5).

My son may choose to flee God's presence in his newfound freedom, but I am thankful God chooses not to let him go.

Kimberly Laliberte uses both head and heart as she practices appellate law and serves on staff at her church as the Director of Adult and Women's Ministries. She is a speaker and Bible teacher and lives with her husband in Southern California.

Sherry Meneley

LIKE A CHILD

EVERY MOMENT COUNTS working as a middle-school ministry youth leader. The volunteered time feels endless; it's natural to get burned out. Occasionally I get frustrated leading a small group of vibrantly beautiful young girls who giggle and chat the time away without bothering to mention God. But then there are the amazing nights with focused discussion and God's presence is obvious. But middle-schoolers haven't honed the ability to concentrate or show respect. It's probably this very aspect that causes me to love them even more. They are a perfect juxtaposition of quirky, disrespectful, awkward, awesome, exhausting, and inspirational.

One particular night I simply did not want to go. I had run bone-dry of the energy and love required for youth group. Yet something nudged at my heart; out of sheer obedience I dragged myself to the church.

My thoughts and feelings of the evening are still fresh. Sarah, an inquisitive Jewish girl, asked me during the worship music, "Will you help me get saved?"

The music piercing, I had to ask her to repeat what she said. Once I understood, I replied with joyful enthusiastic, "Yes!"

Moments later, my mind started to race. How should I do it? Should I follow the youth leader's guide which makes it harder than it really is? As my mind spun, I thought— *I can't help her get saved. I don't know what to do.* That's what God does. And besides, I didn't think she really meant it.

Sarah had been working me over with hard questions about salvation and heaven for months. But more importantly, she wanted to know about hell. Recently the youth group was told if they weren't Christians going to heaven, then they "are" going to hell. Ah, scare tactics! All youth pastors have done this. This message frightened my girls.

That night my heart and mind heart struggled how to respond to an unsaved twelve-year-old girl about heaven and hell. What happens to her family of a different faith? Why do really good moral people, who aren't Christians, go to hell? I didn't like it. Not one bit. As I answered questions, I stuck with my Sunday school taught truth about heaven and hell. But my approach was candy-coated-salt; not veering from the truth, yet hoping the unsaved girls wouldn't be scared to go to sleep that night.

Between that night of "hell" and the night of Sarah's salvation, we had many remarkable conversations about God. While I was happy she asked me to help her "get saved," I also thought, *Child, you have no idea what you're doing, you're becoming a Christian for the purpose of fire-insurance.*

While I understood my essential role in leading Sarah to Jesus, I was unsettled in doing it.

The worship band rocked on. I mentally processed; wrestled the Spirit. My ears deafened to the noise as a gentle voice pulled me into focus and reminded with candy-coated-salt, "this is how it starts with Me, just roll with this, everyone starts somewhere, you've helped her, now I'll take over from here." The voice was right. Who am I to judge if anyone is ready to become a Christian.

We all start our journey of faith somewhere.

After the humbling honor of helping Sarah "get saved" I felt soothing peace and joy. All I could say was "welcome to the club!"

God dramatically revealed Himself to the girls. After Sarah accepted Jesus, the girls pointed at a cloud formation in the summer sky. It looked like a face. The group believed God was looking down from heaven with pleasure. The girls became giddy and filled with the Holy Spirit. It's a special thing to have wonder, belief, innocence, and to receive the kingdom of heaven like a child (Luke 18:17).

Sherry L Meneley resides in California and partners with her husband at their construction company. She's a leader in her church's student ministry and teaches women's Bible studies. Sherry's devotions and articles have been published in Christian and general markets. Sherry can be contacted through http:\\www.soiledwings.com.

Elise Schneider

HERE I AM, LORD

NO MORE SPEAKING requests!" I said to the walls of my office.

I'd arrived on a Monday morning before the birds began chirping. *My campus responsibilities need my primary attention,* I thought. *I will get to know the people in the communities later.*

Not only was I the new President of Oxnard College, I was the *first woman president.* Ventura County Community College District, composed of three colleges, hadn't had a women president in their 64 years of existence. Service clubs were clamoring to have me—the new curiosity—be their luncheon speaker. Pastors asked me to talk to their congregations. They'd heard about my faith and how I gave God full credit for opening the door to my Presidency. It is not uncommon for the incoming President to have been recommended by colleagues within their district. However, I knew no one in the district or county.

Sandy, my assistant, buzzed announcing, "Joy Yates on line two."

"Hi Joy."

"Will you be our keynote speaker for the annual Mayors' Prayer Breakfast this spring?" she asked. "This will be a great opportunity for you to meet the movers and shakers of the county."

"Thanks, Joy, but I'm scheduled to represent our college in Japan this spring—perhaps another year."

I ended our conversation and didn't give the invitation another thought. Nor did I pray about it. This was quite uncharacteristic for me relating to an opportunity to share our Lord.

I went home exhausted, fell asleep, and was awakened by God in the wee hours of the morning! Startled, I listened intently as He told me in no uncertain terms I *was* to be the Keynote Speaker at the Mayors' Prayer Breakfast and the title of my presentation was to be "The Power Of Prayer In My Life."

I jumped out of bed. The hands of the clock seemed to barely move as I waited to dial Joy. I thought 7:30 a.m. would never come. At 7:29 a.m. I placed the call.

"Hello?"

"Joy, do you have a speaker yet?"

"No, Elise, I don't." She tried to stifle a yawn.

"I'll do it, Joy." The words flew out of my mouth as if I feared she might reverse her request. "My title is 'The Power Of Prayer In My Life.'"

"Oh that's wonderful."

"Thanks," I hung up, excited to be following God's clear call to me.

I'd never experienced anything like this—not only had God told me to speak, but He had even given me the topic. "Hallelujah and oh my goodness," I exclaimed. "I'm so excited but what in the world am I going to say?"

I quickly opened my Bible searching for guidance from His Word. "There it is! And I found it no time at all."

"Call on me and I will answer you and I will tell you great and mighty things which you do not know" (Jeremiah 33:3 *The Message*).

Thank you, dear God. I'm anxious to learn the specifics of what You and I will present that day. I'm sure the presentation will demonstrate Your love and the power of prayer in my life.

To an audience of 300+ at The Breakfast, I shared numerous events that revealed the power of prayer throughout my life. I concluded with the true story of a severe automobile accident I'd experienced only three days before The Breakfast. My car was totaled; I walked away without a scratch!

Was Satan attempting to block my Breakfast message?

When I arrived home, the day of the accident, I listened to a phone message from Carol recorded at the precise moment my car careened out of control.

"Elise, are you okay? I feel God is telling me you are in deep trouble!"

I later learned another friend was praying for me fifteen minutes before my accident.

God's overflowing love and my obedience to Him began my speaking ministry which continues today throughout the world.

Dr. Elise Douglass Schneider's passion is serving her Lord through Christian speaking and writing. Her higher education profession spanned 30+ years including two community college presidencies. She has two sons, Michael and Stephen, and three grandchildren. Elise resides in Southern California. Visit www.eliseschneider.com and e-mail her at elise@eliseschneider.com.

Lee Warren

WHERE'S THE CARVING KNIFE?

THE FRONT WINDOW was open and Clanci (Mom's cat) sat in her condo feeling the full effects of the cool breeze as it filtered in. The clock said 4:15 p.m. and the sun was going down already. It was that time of year. A red candle flickered on a nearby TV tray and the Cowboys were up on the Seahawks 27-3 in the second quarter.

I rocked back and forth in the same recliner I always sit in at Mom's house, gently petting Clanci—who was within arm's length, still curled up in her condo. The aroma of turkey made a beeline for the living room. The sound of Mom stacking the plates meant it was nearly time to eat.

For the first time in a couple of years, everything seemed settled, normal—at least as normal as life ever gets. And I was thankful—not for normal, but for God's grace that sustained us when life wasn't so normal.

The previous couple of years had been chaotic. My mom had a stroke in 2007, and my family had several other issues to deal with, much like every family does, but when I thought about God's grace on this particular Thanksgiving Day, contentment from on high washed over me.

The candle smelled better, the turkey tasted better, and the breeze flowing through the window reminded me of the Holy Spirit as Jesus described him in John 3:8, "The wind blows where it wishes, and you hear its sound, but you do not know where it comes from or where it goes." The Spirit was having His way with me that day.

During the holidays, I am always reminded of my singleness. I'm not one who generally struggles a lot with being single, but the holidays are harder—probably because I have an ideal in my head about celebrating the holidays with my wife and kids—neither of which I have. Maybe I've seen one too many family pictures on Christmas cards. But on this particular day, God's grace conquered my loneliness. And it reminded me of the job he had put in front of me.

He reminded me of Rebekah's situation in Genesis 24. She was single and serving her nuclear family. Abraham's servant initially met her at the well, where she drew water. After learning the servant needed a place to stay for the night, she invited him to stay at her family's house. Rebekah's brother, Laban, greeted them. Shortly thereafter, they sat down for a meal.

Abraham's servant knew God had orchestrated the events of the day to make it clear that Rebekah would be Isaac's wife. Rebekah already understood this too, but it was time for her family to hear the case.

Some believe Rebekah's father, Bethuel, was incapacitated because Laban was serving as the head of household. That was probably the case, but Bethuel was involved in the decision-making process (see Genesis 24:50).

The point is life wasn't perfect for Rebekah. Her father may have been struggling with his health and judging by her reaction to the marriage proposal, she had been waiting for marriage for a while. It just had not happened for her yet. Until it did, she was doing what I was doing on this particular day—joining her nuclear family for a meal and serving them. It's where she belonged at that point in her life. It's where I belonged too.

God's gentle reminders kept me in the here and now. I climbed out of the recliner and headed for the kitchen.

"Where's the carving knife?" I said. "It's smells like time to eat."

Lee Warren is an author and freelance writer with five books and hundreds of articles in print. He writes for Baptist Press Sports, the Heartland Gatekeeper newspaper in Omaha, and others. He is on staff with CLASSEMINARS and co-owns A Write Start Communications—a company dedicated to helping writers.

Linda Gilden

THE STORY OF THE SHELLS

WHEN I WAS a little girl our family went to the beach every summer for a week. We loved to walk along the beach to pick up shells. Although the South Carolina coast is not known for unusual shells, we got excited over just a small piece of a sand dollar or the tip of a conch shell.

Our schedule included an afternoon nap for all the children. While we rested Mom rested with us and Dad took a walk on the beach or vice versa.

One afternoon after our rest time, we put on our bathing suits, grabbed our sand buckets, and headed back to the beach. It was always a race to see who would find the first shell.

"I found one," shouted my sister.

Running a little farther down the beach, my brother stopped. "Wow! Come look at this shell."

My eyes glued to the glistening sand I searched for a treasure. There it was partially sticking out of the sand - the tip of a pure, white sand dollar. I carefully dug around the edges. This was the biggest piece of a sand dollar I had ever seen except in the windows of those shell stores downtown.

"Wow!" I said. "This sand dollar is—"

"I found another one."

"Come over here and look at this."

"This sand dollar is *whole*."

My brother, sister and I ran from treasure to treasure. Dad walked silently along beside us. Every time we ran to show him one of our finds, Dad smiled and admired the beautiful shell.

That walk was one of the most memorable, fun times from our beach trips. For years we talked about the beautiful shells.

"Can you believe how many we found?"

"We never saw shells like that again!"

One day recently when all the adult children were together we were having that conversation with my dad yet again. As we went on about what a great harvest of shells we had that particular vacation and how there must have been a tremendous storm at sea for so many to wash up on shore Dad let a giggle escape.

"What's so funny about that?" we asked. "We couldn't believe those shells had washed up there just as we came out to hunt. It was like they were just for us!"

Dad couldn't stand it any longer. "Well, they were." He winked at Mom.

Puzzled looks were all that responded to his comment.

"Do you really think that those whole, unusual shells just happened on the beach that day?" he asked.

"Yes, that's what I thought."

"Me, too."

"Well," Dad said. "I guess I did a pretty good job."

"You what?"

"You didn't really..."

"Yes, that's right. While you were resting, I went down to the shell store. They had some really nice shells. I bought a bag full and just before I came in to get you, I distributed them on the beach, buried some, and took a chance they would still be there when we got outside.

"All these years you let us think we found those all by ourselves?"

"Yes, I wanted you to have the joy of discovering them and showing them off!"

It took years for us to learn the real story of the shells. But once we did, we understood it wasn't just a story about shells. My earthly father had demonstrated to his own children what our Heavenly Father does for us all the time.

His gifts are all around us—we just have to discover the wonderful treasures He has for us. For some it may be a sand dollar. For others, a conch shell. For many, family and friends. For some, treasures may be almost totally hidden from sight and require hard work to find. For all, the greatest treasure is a relationship with Him.

No matter what your treasure, no matter what your gifts, they are waiting for you. And your Heavenly Father waits with anticipation to see you find them. His pleasure and delight in you is evident as He sees you discover something He has put in your path.

I actually think He smiled when Dad went to the shell store!

Linda Gilden is an author, speaker, editor, and writing coach. She is a member of the CLASS training staff, directs the CLASS Christian Writers Conference, and loves to help people learn to communicate. Linda lives in SC with her husband, three adult children, and three grandchildren who love to hunt shells at the beach! www.lindagilden.com

CLASSEMINARS

Training Christian Communicators Around the Globe

Mission Statement

As THE PREMIER Christ-centered trainer of communicators and leaders, CLASSEMINARS, Inc. cultivates, coaches, equips and encourages leaders, authors, and speakers who are committed to living and serving with excellence.

Founded in 1980 by Florence Littauer, CLASS has trained over 30,000 communicators all over the world. Continuing the legacy that Florence began, CLASSEMINARS conducts seminars encouraging speakers and authors to take their skills to the next level. The Personality Training Workshops, another CLASS program, have helped thousands understand themselves and their families better and trained many people to conduct similar workshops. Recently CLASS has added one-day workshops on writing and marketing to their schedule with plans to add more this year.

For more information and a current schedule of CLASS events, go to www.classeminars.org.

Rich with history, the Ghost Ranch, located in Abiquiu, New Mexico was given to the Presbyterian Church by Arthur and Phoebe Pack in 1955. The 21,000 acres that comprise the Ghost Ranch were part of a land grant to Pedro Martin Serrano from the King of Spain in 1766. The grant was called Piedra Lumbre which means shining rock.

Ghost Ranch now serves as an ecumenical and interfaith education and retreat facility of the Presbyterian Church (U.S.A.). For more than half a century people have come for spiritual development, to discuss issues of peace and justice, to work together in creation care, to paint and write, to hike and ride horseback, to research globally renowned archeological and fossil quarries, or simply rest and renew their spirits.

The Ghost Ranch is a place where God's presence is evident in the spirit of His people and in the glory of His creation.

Photo by John Thurman

For more information about the Ghost Ranch visit www.ghostranch.org

LaVergne, TN USA
25 February 2011
217791LV00004BA/1/P